THE APPRAISAL INTERVIEW

An approach to training for
teachers and school management

Eric Hewton

Open University Press
Milton Keynes · Philadelphia

Open University Press
Celtic Court
22 Ballmoor
Buckingham MK18 1XW

and

1900 Frost Road, Suite 101,
Bristol, PA19007, USA

First Published 1988. Reprinted 1990

Copyright © Eric Hewton 1988

British Library Cataloguing in Publication Data

Hewton, Eric, *1934–*
   The appraisal interview : an approach to
   training for teachers and school
   management.
   1. Great Britain. Schools. Teachers.
   Performance. Assessment
   I. Title
   371.1'44'0941

ISBN 0–335–09523–2
ISBN 0–335–09522–4 Pbk

Library of Congress Cataloging-in-Publication Data

Hewton, Eric.
   The appraisal interview : an approach to training for teachers and
   school management / Eric Hewton.
       p.   cm.
   Bibliography: p.
   Includes index.
       ISBN 0–335–09523–2   ISBN 0–335–09522–4 (pbk.)
       1. Teachers–Rating of–Study and teaching–England.   2. Teachers–
   –Rating of–Study and teaching–Wales. 3. Interviewing–Study and
   teaching–England. 4. Interviewing–Study and teaching–Wales.
   I. Title.
   LB2838.H45 1988
   371.1'44–dc19   88–19704 CIP

Typeset by Inforum Limited, Portsmouth
Printed in Great Britain by J. W. Arrowsmith Limited

Contents

This book owes much to the research project on School-Focused Staff Development funded by The Economic and Social Research Council (ESRC), reference number C00232202

Preface

Like many others involved in education, I did not approve of the idea of appraisal in schools when it was first mooted by Sir Keith Joseph a few years ago. It seemed a rather vindictive tool borrowed from industry to be thrust upon a generally demoralized teaching force which was becoming increasingly angry about pay, conditions, status, resources, negotiating rights and an excessive amount of change in too short a time. But I have gradually changed my view. I now believe that appraisal, if used properly, can be a force for good. It can benefit the individual teacher and the school, and such benefits should ultimately help to make education better for the pupils.

Why did I change my mind? The primary reason was because I became involved with helping to think through plans for appraisal schemes in a number of schools. Alongside this activity and supporting it, were discussions on wider policy issues with LEA officers and teachers' association representatives – at first in East Sussex and later in other authorities.

This involvement in the appraisal scene came about rather unexpectedly. Between 1985 and 1987 I co-directed, with Bob Garner of East Sussex LEA, an ESRC-funded project concerned with school-focused staff development. Schools involved in the project were required to produce policies and programmes for staff development based upon a careful analysis of needs – both those of the school and the individual teacher. One way of identifying these was for someone to talk to each teacher about what they saw as their own and the

school's development needs for the future. As those represent-
ing each school on the project began to engage in, what came
to be known as 'staff development review', it became clear
that what was taking place was a form of appraisal.

I say a *form* of appraisal because there is not just one
approach but several, and by concentrating on staff development as the main purpose, a particular model began to emerge
which, as it happened, corresponded fairly closely to the one
that was then being advocated by the ACAS working party on
appraisal.

Those interviews which took place early on during the
project seemed to produce positive responses from teachers.
They enjoyed the idea of being consulted about the needs of
the school and being offered the chance to talk about their own
professional development. Such discussions often touched
upon such matters as past performance, areas of satisfaction
and concern, constraints such as lack of support or resources,
communication difficulties, targets for the future and, in fact,
most of those issues which might be expected to arise in any
fully fledged appraisal scheme. The key point, however, was
that these were associated, in the minds of those concerned,
with the positive purpose of staff development rather than
with any negative or punitive aim such as the often quoted
view that appraisal is for 'weeding out the weak teacher'.

Schemes which began as a voluntary experiment with a few
people involved soon had many others asking to be included.
This was a good beginning, but the 'appraisers' very quickly
recognized the complexity of the process in which they had
become involved. They felt it was something they would like
to do better and also feared that the time could come when
they would make a costly mistake. They began to ask for
guidance and training.

At the time there was a growing literature on appraisal but
very little on appraisal training. Certainly no member of the
project team had any experience in this area, and inquiries
indicated that the education profession as a whole lacked
expertise and resources to provide the training that would
clearly become necessary if, as seemed likely, appraisal was to
become a necessary part of the life of every school.

Industry and commerce, however, seemed to have on offer considerable experience in this field, and it was to a firm of consultants who provided such training that the team first turned. This began a long and fascinating departure into a new training field, some of the outcomes of which are recorded in this book. The path led from complexity to simplicity, from the use of sophisticated video technology to paper and pencil, from role-play to self-evaluation. In this journey 'necessity was the mother of invention'.

Two incidents are worth recalling. The first, at Sussex University's residential centre, involved the use of five video cameras and associated play-back facilities. The training group, mainly heads and deputies, were to role-play appraisers and appraisees on the basis of a scenario provided for the purpose. Their interviews were to be recorded and discussed. A technician was specially brought in from the University's media service unit to set up the equipment, check it and make sure that it operated correctly when the workshop started. I was there an hour before the start to see that everything was in order. No problems arose – not until, that is, the near-by electricity substation was struck by lightning just as the interviews were about to commence. It took most of the day for the Electricity Board to reconnect the supply. Perhaps it was an 'act of God', but whatever the cause, it proved the point that a successful appraisal workshop could be run without the aid of video equipment.

The second incident involved the use of role-play as the basis for practice interviews. I can remember late one evening sitting with three colleagues around a table in the library in a comprehensive school in East Sussex trying desperately to fit the plans for a two-day training programme into one day. The project team had got itself into the position of having offered to do its, by then, standard workshop on appraisal for another LEA only to find out, too late, that only one day was available. Should we withdraw our offer? It was decided that this was not an option and that we had to rethink the entire plan. I can remember suggesting that we drop the role-play process and 'go for real'. In other words, we should ask the participants to 'play themselves' in the interview situation and complete a form which would give the interviewer sufficient information on which to conduct the appraisal. At the time, this seemed a considerable risk, but it worked reasonably well (although I would not recommend a one-day workshop) and has since been developed and refined. It forms the basis of the method described in the following chapters.

There is a lot more yet to be learnt about appraisal training. The more I am involved, the more I am convinced that appraisal has the potential to represent, in microcosm, nearly all management practices – good or bad. It involves evaluating the past and planning for the future, knowing staff as individuals and caring about them, encouraging and facilitating better practices, recognizing constraints on good performance and finding ways of removing them, reconciling conflicting interests and needs and generally making the best use of limited resources. These are, or can be, all reflected in good appraisal procedures. To learn to appraise, therefore, is to learn good management. This is no small undertaking.

The learning process for me has involved other members of the project team. Ruth Adkins, Chris Cornell, Ruth Downer, Bob Garner, Roy Grigg, Tony Howarth, Sylvia McConville, Alan Thwaites and Tony Ward. Ruth, Chris and Sylvia were particularly involved in breaking new ground on self-evaluation, and Tony Ward and Bob Garner have been regular working companions and innovators before and since. I am greatly indebted to them all. I hope this description and expansion of our work will prove useful to others. My thanks also to Tony Becher who read the draft and made several helpful suggestions.

Chapter 1

Introduction

The ACAS agreement between teachers' associations and employers on Appraisal and Training (ACAS 1986) states that 'the entire teaching force will be trained for the introduction of appraisal and resources will be made available for that purpose'. As a part of the agreement, the government has funded six pilot schemes in Croydon, Cumbria, Salford, Somerset, Suffolk and Newcastle in which the LEAs concerned will introduce and monitor appraisal schemes. A National Steering Group has been set up to co-ordinate the pilot LEAs and a separate evaluation project has also been funded. Planning and development work is already underway and, in accordance with principle 7(iv) of the ACAS Agreement, appraisal will normally require an interview conducted by a teacher's immediate supervisor – 'who may be the Head, or other experienced teacher designated by the Head'. The pilot LEAs are now in the process of organizing schemes mostly along these lines. The DES-sponsored Suffolk Project (Graham 1987) recommends that 'Training in appraisal techniques' should become part of each authority's management training programme.

Quite apart from this national initiative, many schools across the country have already introduced, or are about to proceed with, appraisal schemes (Turner and Clift 1985). Several LEAs are also in the process of preparing policies or guidelines pending the introduction within the next year or two of a central directive on appraisal based upon the outcome of the pilot schemes. These schools and authorities are concerned about the implications for resources and expertise of training for appraisal.

Who the book is for

The book is intended for those who have the task of planning and providing a training workshop on appraisal skills. This might include officers and advisers at LEA level, heads or other members of management teams in schools and colleges or their departments, staff development co-ordinators wherever they are based and those in universities, polytechnics or colleges involved in teacher in-service education and training.

What the book is about

The book is primarily about providing practice interviews simply and effectively. In industry and commerce a growing number of managers and other employees are familiar with such interviews and most can claim first-hand experience as either appraiser, appraisee or both (Long 1986). This is not the case in education where, for most teachers, appraisal is an unfamiliar and threatening idea. What happens in an appraisal interview, therefore, is a matter of some concern, and heads and teachers want to know how to approach this new experience. How should the interview be conducted? What skills are required? Is it different from other forms of interviewing (such as for selection, counselling, or research)? Training should provide answers to these questions and above all enable those involved to gain some practice before taking part in real interviews in their own schools.

The book details an approach to training pioneered originally by the School-Focused Staff Development (SFSD) project in East Sussex funded by the ESRC (Hewton 1988). The ideas were later used by members of the team in several other LEAs. Although the project was concerned mainly with school policies for staff development, it was soon realized that appraisal was an important means of assessing staff development needs. Members of the project who started interviewing their staff began to appreciate the high levels of skill that were involved. It was therefore decided to organize a series of workshops in which various approaches to training would be tried. All methods were found to have advantages and disadvantages, but after several workshops over the space of a year one was found which appeared to satisfy many learning needs and to be reasonably simple and economical in terms of time and instructor cost.

The approach is described in detail in the following chapters. Briefly it entails practice interviews conducted in groups of four people. The interview is based upon information contained in a self-evaluation pro-forma completed by all participants beforehand. The rationale behind this particular approach is now explained.

Practice interviews: problems and possibilities

Interviewing, like most other skills, requires practice in order to learn. There is, of course, much that can be taught through the provision of information or by discussion and demonstration, but eventually appraisers must interview in order to improve their techniques, their understanding of what the process is about and ultimately their effectiveness as managers. However, the best way to gain initial practice in the skills of interviewing presents some problems.

Ideally, practice should take place in a real situation or as close to it as possible. To draw an analogy, the would-be golfer has, at some time, to stand on the actual tee, hit the ball and avoid the trees, bunkers and other hazards. The potential appraiser, at some point, has also to come face to face with the possible hazards of interviewing a member of staff. To spoil a shot and lose a golf ball is annoying: to make a mess of an interview and possibly lose the support, motivation or goodwill of a member of staff is serious. The novice golfer is likely to practice beforehand on a driving range or possibly have lessons with a professional in order to approach the first tee with greater confidence. The would-be appraiser is well advised to seek the equivalent of a practice range and feedback from a trusted person. But where can these be found?

Practice with a colleague

One possibility is to seek out a sympathetic and trusted member of staff at school and to try an appraisal interview – followed by discussion and feedback. Some participants at the East Sussex workshops were fortunate enough to have had this experience and found it helpful, but they expressed the view that some structured interview training was also necessary and felt that this should have preceded their own practice sessions in school. The reasons given were that the training indicated to them the importance of understanding the purpose, nature and structure of an appraisal interview and also alerted them to the skills necessary and the potential dangers of ignoring certain basic rules. The practice gained in the relatively safe workshop situation was for them important and valuable.

Case study and role-play

Once practice is taken from the real situation, it becomes, to some extent, false. Simulations involving case studies require people to adopt roles and to act acccording to their interpretation of how someone else might behave in a given situation. The process is sometimes criticized on the grounds that it feels unreal and, for some, embarrassing. Nevertheless, case studies involving role-play are a widely used method of training in industry and commerce.

A workshop using case study materials was organized for the SFSD project team by management consultants Packard and Slater on the lines of the method described in their book *Staff Appraisal* (Randell, Packard and Slater 1984). The case study used sets the scene for a difficult appraisal meeting between a manager and subordinate in the sales department of a manufacturing firm. Considerable details are provided of the problems and perceptions of the parties involved, and the practice interviews are based upon this information.

An evaluation of the workshop by the heads, deputies and teachers forming the project team indicated some degree of satisfaction. The method was generally perceived as enjoyable, the interviews were taken seriously and a good deal of learning took place. But there were other aspects to be considered. The case study itself was complicated and involved the participants in considerable study in order to gain some understanding of the situation in which they were to play a part. There were numerous names to master and facts to remember as well as interpretations of actions to be worked out. This took time but also led to some uncertainty and a feeling of anxiety during the interviews. Several people commented that the industrial setting was too far removed from school life, and they found difficulty in transferring the lessons learnt from the one situation to another.

On the basis of this feedback two relatively simple school case studies were written by members of the SFSD project team. One of these, set in an imaginary primary school but based upon a problem which had actually occurred in one school, is included in Appendix II by way of example. A workshop was then organized on the lines of the industrial model previously tried but using these educationally based case studies. It proved reasonably successful with the project team, but again there were criticisms of the method. Some participants complained of the artificiality which surrounded the interviews. The situations were recognized as being real but they found themselves unable to enter fully into the problem and some felt, throughout, that they were merely acting. This, they maintained, hindered their learning about appraisal. They were prepared to accept role-play in short exercises (some of which are described in Chs. 4 and 5) where a particular point was being demonstrated, but in the longer and generally much more intense appraisal interview situation it seemed far less satisfactory.

This problem has been met on several occasions in training

workshops for purposes other than appraisal. Some people are simply not happy engaging in role-play situations, and their resistance unsettles others and inhibits their own learning. It certainly raises a major barrier to the use of case study and role-play in appraisal training situations. The problem is also compounded by a resistance to the whole idea of appraisal by some teachers and a certain cynicism about the motives of government and LEAs in pressing forward with appraisal schemes. If this is coupled with the time factor – first, people feeling that they have more important things to do in the time available and, second, workshops dealing with complex issues having to be crammed into a small space of time – it is clear that the method used has to be very carefully considered. Case study may be acceptable in industry and commerce because both the resistance problem and the training time factor are generally not as severe. In education a different approach may be necessary which engages more with a feeling of reality.

Building-in 'reality'

It was shortly after this workshop that the SFSD team was asked to provide appraisal training in another county as part of an INSET course on the broader topic of staff development. The time allowed for this was from 10 am to 5 pm on one day. The unsatisfactory experience with case studies and the even more restricted time now available caused a fundamental rethink of the problem of how to provide interviewing practice that was both interesting and relevant.

The participants were all to be heads of departments in secondary schools but each from a different school. They would all have something in common – the general nature of an HoD's job – but the context and specific problems for each person would differ from school to school. The idea that they should somehow interview each other about their actual work seemed sensible, but how far could an interview proceed without the appraiser knowing something of the actual work situation and problems of the interviewee? Non-directive interviewing, in which the interviewee is encouraged to identify and work through his or her own problems (an approach referred to again in Chs 4 and 5), has something to commend it in this situation, but it is a very skilled method and was generally felt by the workshop planners to be a high-risk strategy, especially with only very limited time during the day for explanation and discussion.

What was needed was a means by which those involved in the practice could quickly and easily obtain information about those to be interviewed. It was suggested that an interview pro-forma (various types of which were already used by a number of schools in real appraisal situations) might, at least partially, solve this problem. Many of these forms (which have to be completed by an appraisee before an interview) ask for similar information, and all require the person concerned to think seriously about their job and to write down responses to a number of questions.

The SFSD planning group therefore decided to modify a form used by one of the East Sussex schools and to ask all participants in the workshop to complete it. This would then be used as the basis for a practice interview. It was felt that, adopting this approach, those interviewed would be talking about their own work and future development and would be likely to take the exercise seriously. This proved to be the case and, on this and other occasions since, when the method has been used, participants have referred to the sense of reality and sincerity which have pervaded the exercise. Although the first workshop, using this approach, proved that the method could work, it also demonstrated that a one-day session was un-satisfactory. More time was needed for preparation prior to the practice interviews.

Assumptions

In the workshop described in the following chapters it is assumed that:

1   Training should be for both appraisers and appraisees and be capable of involving groups of teachers at various stages of their career.

2   Only two days are available. Readers will find sufficient ideas and information throughout the book to build a longer workshop if time and resources are available.
3   At least eight people will attend the workshop and participate fully in the exercises. For reasons that will be explained later, numbers attending should preferably be divisible by four. A maximum number for one trainer to handle, using the format suggested, is twenty, but larger groups are possible if accommodation is available and more than one organizer is involved.
4   In addition to the main room, other rooms (to hold four people) should be available. A group of twenty would need five rooms altogether.
5   Video equipment is not necessary. If it is available, it is possible and valuable to use it, but more time will be needed.

What the book is not about

The book is not specifically about:

the history of appraisal;
the current debate on appraisal; its rationale, purposes, outcomes, political control and so on;
systems of appraisal at school and LEA level;
the preparation and uses of appraisal reports;
the costs of appraisal;
the need for classroom observation and methods of doing this;
although all receive some mention.

These issues may arise at an appraisal training workshop, but there is already a considerable literature available on each, and a bibliography is appended containing some suggested reading for programme organizers and workshop participants.

Use in different situations

The method to be described is ideally suited to workshops

organized away from school – in, for instance, teachers' centres, residential centres, colleges and so on – where people from several establishments can be brought together. The fact that participants do not know each other is not a bar to effective practice interviewing. Indeed, it can be an advantage for two reasons. First, interviewers will not have made prior judgements about the standard of work of those they are interviewing which might otherwise hinder the neutrality of their questioning. Second, there is unlikely to be a previous history of unsatisfactory relationships which might stand in the way of open and frank discussion. Consequently, there is much to be said for mixing the staff of several schools and ensuring that the practice groups do not contain people from the same establishment. Furthermore, a larger workshop group, than can normally be recruited from one school, will also provide economies of scale and thereby reduce the cost of training.

These advantages may not apply if a workshop is organized in, or for, a single school. The problem of 'authority' may also prove a hindrance. How might new and inexperienced members of staff, for instance, feel about being interviewed by the head, a deputy head or a head of a department even in a practice situation? Or, conversely, how might a senior member of staff react to being interviewed by, say, a probationary teacher?

These difficulties are real and must be carefully considered, but they should not prevent the method from being used by individual schools provided they are of a reasonable size, are keen to try and have the full backing of the staff. This sometimes happens when a few members of staff have experienced the method described in this book in a larger, mixed workshop and feel able to explain it to the remainder of the staff in a way that will gain their confidence.

In a large secondary school, for instance, provided the purpose and structure of the exercise are fully understood, it should be possible to avoid any major difficulty by forming practice interview groups from people in separate departments or from different parts of the school. Furthermore, as will be explained in Chapter 2, the pro-formas encourage and enable people to say only what they want to say and what they feel safe in saying about themselves. They are therefore unlikely to reveal things which they might regret later. Furthermore, they need not volunteer to be interviewed if they find themselves in a group which they see as in any way threatening.

A training model

The workshop and the book, although focusing upon the central importance of practice interviews, adopt an approach to training which follows a series of steps. It is possible, and also helpful, to draw an analogy with a cookery book recipe and to describe first the ingredients and then the steps necessary to create an acceptable and nutritious offering!

The ingredients

For twenty participants you will need:

1   A minimum of one but preferably two organizers suitably prepared.
2   One large room to hold twenty-two people and allow them room to move around.
3   Four other, reasonably private, small rooms with four chairs in each.
4   An overhead projector.
5   A blackboard and/or flipchart.
6   One video-player.
* 7   A self-evaluation pro-forma for each participant (see Ch. 2). (Each participant should bring with them four copies of their form unless a photocopier is available on the workshop premises.)
* 8   A covering letter explaining the purposes and use of the pro-formas (see p. 25).
* 9   The cards and handout for the 'purposes of appraisal' activity (see pp. 28–31).
*10   The 'principles of appraisal' task (see p. 32).

*11 Two overhead projectors, transparencies and handouts for explaining the appraisal model which underpins the workshop (see pp. 35 and 37).

*12 An OHP and handout on 'question types' (see pp. 44–6).

*13 An OHP and handout for 'interviewing skills – suggestions' (see p. 48).

*14 Instructions for short interview practice (see pp. 49–50).

*15 Instructions for discussion on controlling interviews (see p. 54).

*16 A video of an appraisal interview (see pp. 56–60).

*17 An OHP and handout regarding effective targets (see pp. 60–2).

*18 A workshop evaluation questionnaire (see p. 70).

(The items marked with an asterisk in the above list may be used or adapted without infringing copyright.)

The ingredients are mixed according to the steps in the model below:

A *Pre-preparation*

B *Workshop*
The context of appraisal.
Skills – attending and directing.
Interview practice.

C *Further activities*

These steps are now considered in turn.

A *Pre-preparation*

This involves the completion of an appraisal interview proforma by every participant. There are several reasons why this is useful and necessary. The activity requires the respondents to stop and think about their work and to make some considered comments about it. This is something that will almost certainly be required of them if and when a fully fledged system of appraisal is introduced nationally. Next, it orientates their thinking towards the workshop: they are much less likely to come completely 'cold' to the event. Finally, the form itself provides an essential element of information in the practice interview.

The preparation and use of the pro-forma is explained in Chapter 2.

B   *Workshop*

The context of appraisal   The context of appraisal will, to a large extent, determine the nature of the interview, and time should therefore be allowed for discussion of this matter. There are two main aspects which should be dealt with. The first concerns the purposes of appraisal, of which there seem to be many. Participants need to think through the implications of adopting different purposes and how these will affect actual practice in schools. Closely allied to purposes are the principles which determine and direct the type of scheme which might be used. These also require careful consideration, and some clarification of these issues is necessary before the members can carry out meaningful appraisal exercises.

The context of appraisal is dealt with in Chapter 3.

Skills   There are many skills involved in appraisal, but for the purpose of the workshop these are divided into two main groups: skills of attending (listening, questioning, summarizing, etc.) and skills of directing (negotiating agendas, structuring, pacing, target setting, etc.).

Some understanding of what is involved in these skills requires information, demonstration and structured exercises. These are dealt with in Chapters 4 and 5.

The practice interviews   The way in which these are organized and the roles of the four members of each group are explained in Chapter 6. Some comments are also made about the final plenary session which follows the practice interviews and about the evaluation of the workshop.

C   *Further activities*

Chapter 7 deals with a number of matters including what participants might do to reinforce and extend their learning. Some further suggestions are also made concerning what other activities might be included in a three-day, rather than a two-day, introductory workshop and what might be covered in more advanced training.

Appendices

These contain references (including videotapes) used in the book, a short annotated bibliography of some other writing concerned with appraisal which may be useful to organizers and an illustratory example of a case study used in an early experimental workshop.

The book in summary

If the terms of the ACAS agreement on appraisal and training are followed, every teacher in the country should eventually receive some training. This is a considerable task, and if it is to be undertaken at all, basic training will almost inevitably have to be limited to two or three days at most. The book draws upon the experience of providing a number of two-day, preliminary workshops on appraisal interviewing and offers guidelines on how this might be done effectively and economically. It is not a specialist book about interviewing skills – there are already many of these to which readers may refer. Rather, it suggests how, with only limited time available, it is possible to make people more aware of the skills involved and to provide some initial practice in appraisal interviewing. The aim is to help teachers to develop further their own skills in this respect with a heightened awareness of the problems and possibilities inherent in the process.

Chapter 2

Preparing for the workshop

In this chapter the pro-forma, which is prepared and sent to participants about a fortnight before the workshop, is described and its use explained. First, though, a few words about the process of form filling may be appropriate.

Detailed forms often have to be completed for purposes such as applying for membership of a club, making an insurance claim, seeking a mortgage, an annual tax assessment and so on. Most forms tend to be left for a time because they are not easily completed. Often, they require facts which are not readily available and some thought regarding the type of answer best suited to the particular situation.

More searching questions usually arise in connection with a job application and associated curriculum vitae. Completing such an application is a complex matter and, indeed, courses are sometimes provided on the subject by careers advisers. The applicant has to look back over a lifetime of experience and pull together a personal history which can be projected forward to match a new set of uncertain demands and responsibilities. Applicants must think about themselves, their past and their future in a careful and profound way if they are to succeed.

The process involved is sometimes called self-evaluation, self-assessment or self-analysis. Some people do it much of the time in a random way as they reflect upon recent experiences. But the activity can be sharpened and deepened if it is associated with probing questions and the need to commit thoughts to paper. This requires reflection which is an important part of clarifying and understanding thoughts and feelings.

The self-reflective writing process is sometimes used in education and training. The writing of autobiographies is now found in a number of courses, particularly English and the humanities (e.g. Abbs 1974). Management training often concentrates upon self-evaluation, and the literature on this subject contains numerous examples of questionnaires which may be used by individuals to probe their thoughts and feelings about all aspects of their work (e.g. Boydell and Pedler 1981; Woodcock and Francis 1982). Some argue that even if the process went no further than serious reflection and writing, this would, still be a valuable exercise (Elliot-Kemp and Rogers 1982).

Preparation for an appraisal interview involving self-evaluation of this kind will almost certainly contribute to the quality of the ensuing discussion. It is for this reason that schools and LEAs which have experimented with appraisal systems have generally used a pro-forma of some kind. The ACAS agreement (ACAS 1986) which underpins the national pilot schemes also offers guidelines on the type of form that might be used.

Choosing a pro-forma

It could be argued that the best pro-formas are those compiled and completed by individuals for themselves, indicating an understanding of professional self-evaluation – not only answering searching questions but also deciding what those questions should be. Perhaps in more advanced workshops this would be feasible, with the task being carried out individually or in groups. But for a two-day workshop the preparation time necessary would be difficult to find.

The organizers will therefore need to look at what is already available. There is no shortage of forms in use – some published, others obtainable from firms, local authorities or educational establishments. They range from a very short, three-

or four-question format, to lengthy and detailed documents. The aim is always to stimulate some thinking about what has happened in the past year and what can be learnt from it in order to promote improvement or development in the coming year.

Industrial and commercial organizations have used such forms for some time and it is worth looking at a typical format used by one large firm.

After a brief introduction detailing the aims of the interview and asking the appraisee to hand the form to the interviewer a few days before the meeting, the following questions are posed:

1   What do you consider to be the main tasks and responsibilities in your work?
2   Consider each main task or responsibility in turn and indicate:

> difficulties or problems you have had;
> suggestions for improving the situation.

3   Have you experienced any difficulty in your working environment or any ill health which may have affected your work?
4   What part of your work do you find most demanding?
5   Is there any area of work in which you feel you might be happier or more effective?
6   Is there any part of your work for which you think further training might help?
7   Are you studying for any examinations or qualifications at present?
8   How do you see your career development over the next three years?
9   List any special achievements in work or outside during the past year.
10   Are there any other matters you would like to discuss?

The SFSD team, when considering this form, felt that it stressed the negative aspects of performance, particularly in question 2, which immediately requires the respondent to dwell on difficulties and problems. Perhaps to avoid the negative connotations, the ACAS agreement (ACAS 1986) suggests a somewhat different format, as follows:

> As part of the annual cycle of teacher performance appraisal you will be able to have a discussion with your head teacher/appraiser about your work during this academic year and your work plan for the coming year. The purpose of this process is to identify needs for the professional growth of all teachers and to promote teacher effectiveness by endeavouring to meet these needs wherever possible.
>
> You may find it helpful to prepare yourself by answering these questions in advance of the interview, although you are not required to make the completed form available to your appraiser if you prefer not to do so.

1 Write down what you think are the main tasks and responsibilities of your current post.
2 During the past academic year, what parts of your job have given you greatest satisfaction? How could these be used to best advantage?
3 What parts of your job have given you least satisfaction? Is there something that could be done to overcome this?
4 Where are there problems or difficulties which prevented you from achieving something you intended or hoped to do? Could they be eliminated?
5 To help improve your performance in your job, what changes in the school organization would be beneficial?
6 What additional things might be done by your headteacher? Your head of department? You? Anyone else?
7 What do you think should be your main target(s) goals for next year?
8 How would you like to see your career developing?

This form is certainly more positive than the one cited earlier and is specifically focused upon the work of the teacher. Some workshop organizers may therefore wish to use this already agreed format which commands general acceptance.

The pro-forma adopted for the SFSD workshops uses a combination of questions from the commercial model and the ACAS form. The intention was to create a questionnaire which concentrates upon the positive aspects of a persons work whilst not ignoring those areas where improvements might be possible. It also seeks to provide additional information to help those to whom the appraisee is not known. Finally it is worded in such a way that it can be used for any group of participants which might include, for instance, entry or professional grade teachers, heads of department, deputy heads or head teachers. The form is set out in full below except that more space for writing would normally be left between questions.

Pre-interview appraisal form

Name

Position

Details of school (Phase, location, size and any special features)

This form is intended to provide important background information for your appraisal interview. It is worth spending some time answering the questions fully and carefully, bearing in mind that the aims of the interview are to consider:

your performance over the past year;
the context within which you have been working, especially ways in which it
    has affected your performance;
your career aspirations;
any other matters you may wish to raise.

Please ignore questions which do not seem relevant to you or which seem
    impossible to answer. Also please feel free to alter the wording of any
    question if this seems appropriate. The form will be returned to you after
    the interview.

1   List your main responsibilities.

2   Are these as defined in your job description? (If not how do they differ?)

3   Consider each main responsibility and state:

(a)   areas in which you are generally satisfied with your performance;

(b)   areas in which you have experienced difficulty and in which you feel that improvements might be made.

4   List those parts of your job that give you greatest satisfaction. Can you give reasons why this is so?

5   Refer to parts of your job that are less satisfying than others. Can you give reasons why this is so?

6   Which parts of your work do you find the most demanding or stressful? Can you explain why this is so?

7   Consider your relationships with the following groups (where relevant) and comment on each:

(a)   your pupils;

(b)   your colleagues;

(c)   those in authority to whom you are responsible within the organization,

(d)   those who are responsible to you;

(e)   others such as parents, governors, etc.

8   What has been your main contribution to the school over the past year?

9   Is there any part of your work for which further education or training would be beneficial?

10   Are you engaged in any form of education or training connected with your work at present?

11   How would you wish to see your career develop in the next three years?

12   What do you see as your key tasks for the coming year? Answer up to six as you wish.
     i

     ii

     iii

     iv

     v

     vi

13   Please add any further comments which should be considered during the interview.

(To be completed at the end of the interview.)
Targets AGREED

Signed
Appraiser

Appraisee

Using the form in a workshop situation

Whether organizers adopt the above form or draw up their own document, they will almost certainly meet some criticism. It seems impossible to produce the perfect document to suit all tastes and all needs. It will be considered by some to be too long and by others too short. Or it will be regarded as too superficial or too complicated. Self-evaluation is clearly a matter of individual opinion. But, this said, participants in past workshops have generally completed the exercise with care and diligence and after the practice interview have usually commented upon its usefulness.

Some points are worth making about the form as it stands, and with these in mind organizers may then feel more confident to design their own form for the particular kind of workshop they have in mind.

There is some factual information to begin and this is useful background for those who do not know the appraisee. The introduction is important in order to explain, or remind the respondent about, the purpose of the form and the interview of which it will form an important part.

Question 1 is seemingly straightforward and factual but for some people it requires careful thought and may necessitate reference to their job description. Thus it is linked to question 2 in order to encourage reflection upon whether the job is still the same as it was when the description was originally drawn up. Some respondents commented that simply answering these two questions led them into renegotiating their job description. A few indicated that they were not sure if they had one at all!

Question 3, building on the answers to question 1, moves straight into positive aspects of the work – those areas where performance is considered satisfactory. This positive approach from the start is important. Most people are satisfied with their performance on the majority of their tasks. This, unfortunately, is seldom acknowledged by themselves or others. It is therefore a useful exercise to be asked to write down these successes. The responses generally fit well with the first part of the interview where the intention is to encourage and to praise.

By comparison, the unsatisfactory performances referred to in question 3 generally add up to only a small list. They are nevertheless significant, if for no other reason than that the respondents themselves are not satisfied. These points will generally be picked up in the second part of the interview. It is, incidentally, surprising how open and honest people are in answering this part of the question.

In question 4, the respondent is asked to think about the good things and feelings associated with the job. Even those who are generally frustrated and pressured can usually find something to remain cheerful about. Some participants in earlier workshops remarked how much they had (unexpectedly) found to be positive in terms of job satisfaction.

The second part of the question asks them to consider reasons why they are satisfied. This often brings out interesting replies which can be explored further in the interview. For instance, one person commenting that pastoral work gave him the most satisfaction, explained that he was much happier working with individuals and small groups and was increasingly being recognized as someone in the school who could council 'difficult' children and their parents. This response led to much further discussion in the practice interview and resulted in an action plan for further professional development which was subsequently implemented.

Questions 5 and 6 refer to the opposite: those areas which

are less satisfying than others or those which are considered to be demanding and/or stressful. It might be possible to combine these two questions, but the intention is to draw a distinction between the two feelings of dissatisfaction and stress. At least it provides the respondent with the opportunity to place on record matters which cause some element of concern. Wherever and however the response is made, it will provide the basis for further careful exploration during the interview.

Question 7 is a difficult one for people to answer and is sometimes ignored or answered in a superficial way – 'OK, good, fine'. This either means that all is well with relationships as far as the respondent is concerned or that this is all he or she is prepared to reveal at this stage. But sometimes the answers are not so positive. 'Bad' in any of the categories is clearly an area of concern, but even 'fair' will indicate to the sensitive interviewer that there is something here that the interviewee may be prepared, or even wish, to follow up.

Question 8 is a good antedote to possible negative replies elicited by earlier questions. The answer requires positive reflection, but replies are often beset by undue modesty. Again the sensitive interviewer may pick up brief comments here and use them as points of discussion in the first part of the interview.

Questions 9 and 10 relate to personal and professional development. Has the respondent any ideas about further education or training and what, if anything, is happening in this field at present? This is again approached in a positive manner. Much that has already been written in the pro-forma may indicate what action is needed here, and the interviewer will be looking for opportunities to build upon earlier discussions to show the way forward. The intention will be to encourage and enable interviewees to build their own plans in this respect.

Question 11 is again looking forward and requires the interviewees to think about the next step(s) in their career. Although there is clearly little practical help that appraisers can give in a practice interview, it is still possible to help and encourage the appraisee to think this through more carefully and test out ideas against those of a (generally) neutral and uninvolved outsider.

Question 12 is important in that it can form the basis for target setting. What are the main tasks for the coming year? 'To establish more and better links with parents' might be the reply of a newly appointed head. Or 'to ensure closer working relationships with colleagues in respect of an integrated module' might be another from a teacher involved in say, BTEC work. The interviewers will want to probe as to how these might be achieved – special meetings, written materials, new structures and so on? The answers to these questions combined with those regarding professional development will be used to refine targets set out at the end.

Question 13 is useful if respondents are frustrated by not being asked for information considered important to them. Some useful clues as to the interviewee's current frame of mind are sometimes given in answer to this question.

Finally, the parties to the interview are asked to state the further action (targets) agreed. This offers some practice in negotiating and provides a foretaste of the problems which might be involved in a real interview. It also raises questions about the nature and purpose of the summary/action plan, and these can be considered in the final plenary session.

Explaining the use of the pro-forma to workshop participants

The first time the SFSD team used this method participants were required to complete their forms as part of the workshop activities. This enabled the organizers to explain the reason for the questionnaires, the benefits to be derived from completing them and exactly how they would be used. The problem, though, was one of time. At least an hour is needed, and many people indicated that much longer should have been allowed. This time is difficult to find in a tightly scheduled workshop. The team therefore decided to plan future events on the assumption that those involved would complete a pro-forma before arriving. This seems to have worked well, but it is important that the matter is fully explained by letter as suggested in the following example.

Enclosed are the papers for the forthcoming appraisal interviewing skills workshop. It will help considerably in covering the various issues and activities if you will complete the pro-forma which is attached. The reasons for this are as follows.

During the workshop you will be involved in a practice interview. This will be a simulation exercise but will be as close to a real appraisal situation as possible. In order to achieve this we are asking all participants to think seriously about their work and to answer the questions on the form as though they were approaching an actual appraisal interview in their own school. Therefore, please give careful thought to your answers and be as full and honest as possible.

One person in every four will be asked to play the part of an appraisee. He or she will be interviewed by three other participants. They will use the appraisee's form as the basis for the interview. From it they will obtain facts and views regarding your work and these will provide the main information around which discussion will centre.

Some of those attending the workshop you will know. But others you will not know and your answers should be sufficiently informative for them. As an appraisee you will be free to expand on the matters mentioned in the pro-forma if you deem it appropriate. The form will be seen only by the three others who will work with you, and it will be returned to you at the end. If you are an appraiser, no one else will see your form.

The selection of appraisees will be on a voluntary basis and you are asked, when returning the form, to indicate whether you would be prepared to be interviewed. But whether or not you become an interviewer or interviewee, the completion of the form is a valuable exercise. Those who have taken part in earlier workshops have commented how helpful they found it to be. The very act of reflecting upon their work and then writing down their thoughts often clarified matters and created ideas for future action. Furthermore, when appraisal becomes an established part of school life, such forms will be regularly used, and it is helpful to obtain a foretaste of the demands they bring and their usefulness. We hope, therefore, that you will enter fully into the spirit of the exercise. It would also help if you would bring three copies of the completed form with you.

Organizers will wish to prepare their own letter according to the workshop format, but the above wording illustrates the kind of points which are helpful to prospective participants. In past workshops all but a few have engaged wholeheartedly in this preparation: some have even shown the form to colleagues and discussed it with them before completing it.

The use of the pro-forma: a summary

The pro-forma is an important part of the workshop but is completed by all participants beforehand. The intention is to encourage those involved to reflect upon their work over the past year and to think through their developmental and career goals for the coming year and beyond. If the questions set out on the form are probing enough and those taking part take the task seriously, the answers will provide most of the information needed by the appraisers in the practice interview. The purpose of the pro-forma should be carefully explained in a letter to all participants.

Organizers may wish to prepare their own form using the ACAS document as a guide. Alternatively, they may prefer to use, or adapt, the form set out in this chapter. Only one out of every four forms completed will be used in the workshop unless it is decided to have a second round of practice interviews. Those who complete a form but do not use it in the workshop normally find the exercise valuable in itself. The forms used in the practice interviews should always be returned to the appraisees at the end of the interview.

Chapter 3

The context of appraisal

This chapter deals with some factual material and supporting exercises which are useful and, in most cases, necessary in opening the workshop. The aim is to involve the participants in thinking about some of the key issues involved in appraisal and particularly its purposes, of which there are several. It can be pointed out to the group that unless such purposes are clear and properly understood by those involved – appraisers and appraisees – there will be both suspicion about the nature of the scheme and confusion regarding its operation. In practice, as the first exercise demonstrates, there exist many different and, often, conflicting views about the purposes of appraisal and their order of priority.

Purposes of appraisal

To begin the workshop it is suggested that, after a brief welcome to the participants and an explanation of the aims and mode of working, any uncertainties and concerns should be heard and discussed. Thirty minutes is allowed for this on the programme but, if there are no major matters to deal with, the first exercise can begin sooner.

Participants are told that the exercise is intended to provoke discussion regarding the many purposes of appraisal and to offer the opportunity for the group as a whole to try to reach agreement on what it regards as the most important of these purposes.

They are divided into groups of six and can work in one large room or in separate rooms. This particular exercise, however, is well suited to one large room because it usually generates much debate and excitement and creates an atmosphere of involvement and purposefulness early on. Each group is provided with an envelope containing twenty small cards (measuring 8 cm × 8 cm). On fifteen of these there is written a statement regarding a possible purpose of appraisal such as 'to identify staff development needs' or 'to provide evidence for salary increase or promotion'. The other five cards are blank. Also provided is a large card (24 cm × 24 cm) divided into nine equal squares. Groups are asked to use the card as a diamond shape – which means that one square is at the top (Fig. 3.1) – and to place nine of their cards in priority order on the matrix. They may use the statements as provided or construct their own.

The handout, shown below, is distributed with the cards. This sets out some background information regarding the government's plans to introduce appraisal into the education system and the current position. It then describes the task which participants are required to complete. Organizers will

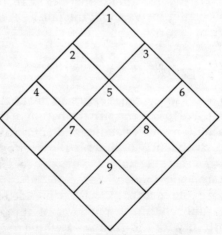

Figure 3.1 *The purposes of appraisal: the card used for a group task.*

need to update the background material from time to time as the national scene changes. They may also wish to modify or add to the statements on the cards. Ten minutes will be required to explain the exercise and for the participants to read the handout.

The purposes of appraisal: background and task

Appraisal formally appeared on the education scene about 1983 as part of a general move towards greater accountability in the service. The DES publications *Teaching Quality* and *Better Schools* clearly indicated the government's intention to introduce teacher appraisal. Reactions from the teachers' associations were generally positive until the issue became enmeshed in the negotiations over pay and conditions. The dispute was eventually referred to the Advisory Conciliation and Arbitration Service (ACAS), and in January 1986 it was agreed to set up a special working group on appraisal training. Its first report was published in June 1986 (ACAS 1986) and indicated broad agreement on the form which appraisal might take. It was recommended that a pilot study, directed by a National Steering Group (made up of teachers' associations, LEAs and DES representatives), should be set up to test procedures and documents. In August 1986 all LEAs were invited to make bids for involvement in the pilot study for which funding would be provided by the DES. Schemes were eventually accepted from six LEAs – Croydon, Cumbria, Salford, Somerset, Suffolk and Newcastle upon Tyne.

Most of the teachers' associations currently take the view that development work on the pilot schemes should proceed, but until such time as agreement is reached on the wider issue of negotiating rights concerning pay and conditions, participation should fall short of actually taking part in the appraisal process. Development work therefore seems likely to proceeed with either the full or tacit support of the teachers and their associations, but there are many issues still to be resolved, not least the purpose of appraisal. Unless the purpose is clear, it is difficult to see how schemes can be properly formulated and interviews conducted in a form which is understood and accepted by those concerned.

The exercise set out below will seek to elicit the views of participants on the crucial issue of purpose(s) and the following points will be of help in preparing for this.

1 The statements below have been suggested by various writers as the main purposes of appraisal:

checking and monitoring teacher performance;

    providing profiles of staff for the record;

    allocating rewards through salary adjustments and promotions;

    planning future staffing requirements;

    assessing the potential of individuals;

    providing information on unsatisfactory teachers;

    ensuring improved standards in the classroom;

    making teachers properly accountable;

    improving managers' knowledge of their staff;

    identifying staff development needs;

    the opportunity for staff to make their views known on matters of concern;

    an opportunity to praise staff for their performance;

    as an aid to writing references;

    to set targets for the coming year;

    to identify problems shared by the teacher and the school.

2   Most agree that appraisal cannot achieve all of these ends at the same time, and some regard certain purposes as unacceptable.

3   There is considerable debate as to where the emphasis should be placed. The teachers' associations generally favour a definition which stresses development of the individual, for example 'a systematic review of performance and potential as part of a full scheme of personal and professional development'. But, from a management standpoint, it is argued that this does not take into account the needs of the client, the school and the LEA. The management of schools is inevitably concerned to ensure that teachers perform effectively as part of a team or a system? Schools and LEAs are accountable to their clientele and to a wider public for the standard of education which they provide. Appraisal is regarded as a necessary part of discharging this responsibility.

4   There are, it seems, two, main, underlying philosophies: one stresses professional development, the other emphasizes accountability, and they lead in different directions. The former will be concerned with the development needs of the individual teacher, appropriate INSET activities, providing broad-ranging work experience, career counselling, job satisfaction concerns, and so on. The latter approach, concerned more with accountability, will concentrate upon the assessment of standards. It will be linked to the overall evaluation of a school's performance, the needs of the school as an organization and the discharge of its responsibilities towards its clients – effectively and efficiently.

5   ACAS faced with the task of reconciling these two standpoints made the following statement:

    appraisal should be a continuous and systematic process intended to help individual teachers with their professional development and career planning and ensure that the in-service training and deployment of teachers matches the complementary needs of individuals and their schools.

It will be noted that the needs of the individual and the school are here linked.

Task

In the task that you will now begin you are asked to place in rank order nine of the fifteen statements about the purposes of appraisal which appear in point 1 above. These are written on cards, and you should place them on the board provided in the order of importance accorded to them by the group as a whole. As the board is diamond shaped, it requires you to place one card above all the others. This then becomes your overriding aim. In case you feel that the wording on any of the cards is inappropriate or you think of another purpose which is not included, you may write a new statement on the blank cards. You have forty minutes.

Organizers should warn the groups five minutes before their time is up. Each group can be asked to lay their completed card out on a large table and a few minutes can be allowed for members to look at the priorities of the other groups.

The whole exercise should take about one hour. This will leave fifteen minutes for discussion when a number of points might be considered, for instance:

1 Did the participants find it easy to reach agreement in their groups? Groups generally find it quite difficult to obtain consensus.
2 If it was difficult, what was the reason? Some people blame the cards, despite the fact that they had the option to make their own. Others do not like the diamond shape and cannot agree that there should be one overriding purpose. But mostly there are disagreements about what an appraisal interview should seek to achieve. This is particularly so where the groups contain a mixture of people from different positions of authority within their schools. In other words, a junior teacher may see quite different purposes for appraisal from, say, a head teacher.

3   If there is uncertainty, or, worse, disagreement about the purpose(s) of appraisal what will be the likely consequence during an interview? Participants should be asked to consider and comment upon this. Replies will normally illustrate the point that a shared sense of purpose is essential if appraisal is to be seen as a force for good and an effective means of improvement within the school.

At this point it is useful to break, but before members leave for coffee it can be helpful to give them prior warning of the task which they will be asked to undertake when they return. This often generates discussion during the break period. The task which they come back to is:

List the four main principles which you would want to see underpinning an appraisal scheme in your own school. You have ten minutes.

Principles of appraisal

Each person takes ten minutes to write down their four principles. The 'snowball' method is then used to share ideas and require further thinking. Individuals form pairs for ten minutes and between them reduce their combined, eight principles to four only. Then the pair joins with another pair and again they reduce their combined, eight principles to four. Finally a group of eight undertakes the same task, to agree four fundamental principles which they would seek in an appraisal scheme in their own school.

Each group of eight should then write their four statements on a board or flipchart. Alternatively, they might prepare an overhead projector transparency, but this normally requires a projector for each group so that the agreed principles can be viewed at the same time by all. Altogether the task should take forty-five minutes.

There is no magic in the number 4, but it has been found in past workshops to be an appropriate figure which requires participants to be specific about their main values in connection with appraisal.

A typical list might be:

1 The purposes of the scheme should be understood and agreed by all members of staff.
2 The main purpose should be staff development.
3 The head should be the first to be appraised.
4 The interview and the report produced as a result should be confidential.

Another list might adopt different principles, for example:

1 The primary purpose should be to improve the education of the pupils.
2 The head should carry out all interviews.
3 The head should see the appraisee actually teaching at least twice.
4 Evidence collected for the interview should be available to both parties.

Seldom are lists the same, either between groups or from one workshop to another. But what they help to do is raise issues about appraisal and demonstrate beyond any doubt that it is a complex process underpinned by important value positions which need to be discussed and clarified if serious misunderstandings are to be avoided. About ten minutes should be allowed for discussion, and during this time one of the organizers should list on the board the key, unresolved questions. The list will probably include some or all of the following:

Who should do the interviewing?
How many people can one appraiser be reasonably expected to interview?
How often should interviews take place?
When (in the day, term or year) should they take place?
How long should they normally last?
Should the appraiser always see the appraisee teaching?
To what extent should the appraisee prepare for the interview?
Should an agenda be agreed beforehand?
What about the really weak teachers; will their interview be different?
Should you deal with personality matters if you feel that they lie at the root of the problem?

Should you allow or encourage the appraisee to criticize you
   or other members of staff?
What will be the effect of taking notes in an interview?
Who should write the report?
What should the report contain and how long should it be?
Should it be confidential to the two parties?
And so on.

There is practically no end to the number of questions that
may be raised by the discussion, and in a two-day interviewing workshop the group must be content to accept that most
are difficult issues on which some agreement was reached in
the ACAS negotiations or are still under review within the six
pilot schemes. It seems that some time must elapse before a set
of guidelines is agreed nationally, but it is important to be
aware of the problems which still exist at this time.

But the matter cannot simply be left there if participants are
to carry out their own practice interviews. They will already
have established that an effective interview must be set within
a framework of purposes and values. To interview properly
they should have such a framework, and the organizers must
provide this. It can be pointed out that the model to be
provided is only one amongst several but that it contains many
of the principles of the ACAS agreement and offers a generally
acceptable approach which brings together the needs of the
school and those of the individual teacher.

An appraisal model for the practice interview

The following principles can be explained and discussed within the thirty minutes left in this session. The main points can
easily be incorporated in a handout or on overhead projector
transparencies.

1   There are, or should normally be, two developmental
    processes going on within a school throughout its life. One
    is the responsibility of management and concerns the
    development of the school as an organization, including
    those who work within it. The second relates to the

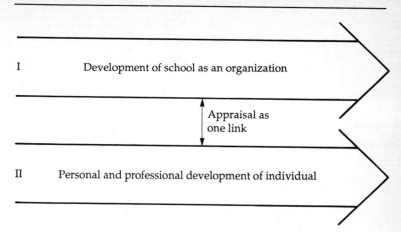

I   Development of school as an organization

Appraisal as
one link

II   Personal and professional development of individual

Figure 3.2 *The development processes*

professional development of each teacher, and this is, primarily, the responsibility of the individual concerned. These two processes can be illustrated by a diagram (Fig. 3.2).

The management responsibility is towards the school as a whole and is concerned with such matters as curriculum development, improvements in teaching and learning, communication, relationships, morale, efficiency, policy-making and so on. Each individual, as a professional, is responsible for his or her own development – in terms of knowledge, performance and career advancement. But, in addition, each person might reasonably be expected to see their own development in relation to the present and emerging needs of the school and the departments within it.

Thus management has two main responsibilities in this respect: first, the development needs of the school as a whole and, second, the needs of each member of staff within it. Alongside these responsibilities the individual will, first, be concerned with his or her own needs and, second, with the needs of the school.

Both sets of responsibilities relating to development

should, it might be argued, be primarily, if not exclusively, concerned with improving the educational experiences of the pupils.

2   Throughout the on-going life of the school there will be a continuous process of explicit or implicit negotiation in which management and individual members of staff make these needs known to each other and place some value and priority on what is said. Communication on these issues may take place at any time in formal or casual conversations – in an office, a corridor, classroom, committee or staffroom. These interactions are represented by vertical arrows in Figure 3.3. If the communication is regular and open, many problems which might otherwise fester will be dealt with promptly and without too much fuss. In addition, those involved will attain a clearer picture of the needs of others. If communication of this sort is poor, then the school may well find an increase in the number of difficult problems, relationship difficulties and crises.

Into this communication network it is possible to introduce an appraisal system based upon formal interviews. Perhaps, to use two metaphors, it might be described as 'a punctuation mark in the on-going conversation within the school' or as 'time out' of the normal hurly-burly of the school day or year (Fig 3.3).

The point to stress in all of this is that appraisal is not something exceptional and exclusive, but rather that it is, or should be, part of the on-going process. The short vertical arrows represent regular communication. The interviews, shown as circles, are an addition to the regular process and, as such, if properly conducted, should improve the flow of information and lead to better understanding.

3   The interview itself is also part of an appraisal process which involves a preparation stage and a follow-up period. Furthermore, it is part of a series of interviews which, through reports and targets, will be linked to each other over time. The second interview will build upon the first and so on. Preparation means the collecting of information

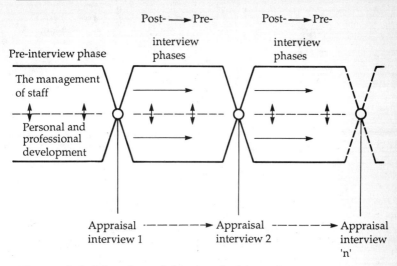

Figure 3.3 *The place of the appraisal interview*

by both parties and the prior setting of agendas. Follow-up means supporting and monitoring progress on any targets that are agreed and set for the coming year.

4   The focus of the interview should be progress and problems as they affect the school and the individual. The interview is thus a joint, monitoring and problem-solving activity in which the peformance and development needs of the individual are considered in the wider context of the school. No problem is without its context, and this is an essential principle of an appraisal interview. If individuals experience difficulties in their work, then these are normally, better discussed, not in personal terms but as part of a problem which the school as a whole must face and solve. It may well be that in some cases it is the management, rather than the individual, that needs to set new targets and goals in order to improve an unsatisfactory state of affairs.

5   This approach leads to the following definition of appraisal. Appraisal is about:
    (a) identifying areas in which the school might improve

the services which it offers to its clients and its staff, and

(b) agreeing what action should be taken towards this end by the organization as a whole and by all individuals working within it.

The above points and accompanying definition seem to be generally acceptable to most participants. But it can again be emphasized that it creates a model which is 'middle of the road'. It is not a pure personal/professional development approach nor is it an accountability model, rather it incorporates elements of both. Whether it is an approach that will ultimately survive in the national debate is of less importance in the present context than that a set of principles are available for participants to work from. Thus, when they enter the room to undertake the practice interview the roles and expectations of the appraiser and appraisee should be reasonably clear.

The appraiser will represent the needs of the school and be concerned to help the appraisee develop as an individual and member of a team towards satisfying such needs. Where the needs of the individual and the school appear to diverge, clarification and negotiation may be necessary. The appraisee will reflect upon performance and put forward his or her own needs in the context of the school as a whole. How best to conduct the interview in order to achieve these intentions is the subject of the next two chapters, which deal with the workshop sessions on interviewing skills.

Summary

This chapter deals with the important opening session of the workshop which is concerned with the purposes and principles of appraisal. Some background information regarding the current position nationally is provided in a handout, and participants are then required to carry out an exercise which requires them to rank, in priority order, a set of suggested purposes of appraisal. Following discussion of the outcomes the group then undertakes a further task in which members attempt to agree upon a number of key principles which should underpin an appraisal system. Both tasks are meant to raise issues and to indicate the extent of competing values which still surround the whole appraisal debate.

A model of appraisal based upon the notion of joint problem-solving is then put forward as a framework within which participants should carry out their practice interviews. It is stressed that this is not the only model available but that it is one that has been found to be generally acceptable to management and teachers and which provides a reasonably clear role for both parties within the interview situation.

Chapter 4

Interviewing skills I

The skills of effective interviewing are many and complex. There is a considerable literature on the subject (e.g. Bessell 1971; Cross 1974) and training courses for professionals, particularly those in the caring services such as social work, guidance counselling and so on can last for weeks or even months. In the context of training for appraisal interviewing, the skills needed are also complex, but the time available in an introductory workshop of this kind is limited. The aims of the sessions devoted to these skills therefore must, of necessity, be modest. They are:

to raise awarenesss of the key issues and skills which underlie effective interviewing and

to equip the participants with sufficient knowledge and techniques to approach the practice interview with confidence and the desire and ability to learn from the experience.

Important aspects of a teacher's work are the possession of (often specialized) knowledge, the ability to convey information clearly and in an interesting way, and the skills of managing and holding the attention of a large group of young people. These, together, demand at least an appearance of confident authority and control. Most teachers, even if well versed in learner-centred, exploratory modes of teaching, bring their authoritative style of communication to the interview situation. In other words, there is a tendency to tightly control the interview, to ask pre-prepared questions, to do much of the talking, to seek to identify the appraisees' problems and to tell them how to overcome them.

There may be some periods in an appraisal interview when these skills might be required, but what is also needed is the ability to listen and to draw out from the interviewee essential information. In other words, the balance should be shifted away from interviewer dominance towards creating space for the interviewee to think through ideas and express them without the feeling of being boxed in by questions and the preconceived notions of others.

Thus, what is needed by teachers involved in training for appraisal interviewing is:

a reminder (for many know this already) that careful listening or attending is important and

a demonstration of the skills involved together with an illustration of their effectiveness if sensitively used.

A technique which is useful in this respect is microcounselling (Ivey and Gluckstern 1977). The books and manuals which describe this approach amount to a substantial and detailed literature, but the essence is incorporated in a useful paper by Hobbs (1987). It is partly from these sources that the following ideas and exercises on attending skills are derived.

Three basic microcounselling skills are:

listening and encouraging the interviewee to talk,
using appropriate questions and
paraphrasing and summarizing.

Here these will be taken in turn to form the basis for a package of inputs, demonstrations and exercises which have proved helpful in preparing for the main practice interview.

Listening and encouraging the interviewee to talk

Listening is far from a passive exercise. It involves not only hearing what is said but also judging what is meant by the words and accompanying body language. It relies upon visual as well as aural information. Watching an interviewee's face, body posture and movements; and attention to verbal cues such as rapid speech, hesitancy, stammer, repetition, sharp breath, tone of voice, overlong silence and so on may be of equal importance as the actual words used by interviewees when forming judgements about their actual meaning.

It is useful to begin this session with a warm-up exercise which focuses attention upon listening skills. Virtually any topic which enables one person to talk freely and easily and the other to listen is appropriate. For instance:

In pairs, one person to talk for two minutes about the place where they were born whilst the other listens carefully and gives full attention. Then reverse roles. After the exercise pairs can be asked to comment to the other upon how it felt to be listened to entirely without interruption and whether the listener 'heard' anything beyond the actual words used. The time for this exercise and discussion should not exceed ten minutes.

The next exercise should attempt to raise awareness about the skills of attending and the problems that some people have in actively listening and concentrating on what is being said. Again, the topic can be chosen from a wide range of possibilities, for instance:

In threes, one person to volunteer to be interviewed for three minutes about their most vivid learning experience (as a teacher or student). A minute should be allowed for the interviewee to recall such an experience. One person then conducts the interview in any way he or she pleases whilst the third member of the group observes and makes notes. Allow five minutes for the groups to discuss any significant factors about the interview which occur to them, including how the participants felt during the process. It is possible for the organizer(s) to sit in on a group as an extra observer. The process should take ten minutes.

This exercise provides the basis for a fifteen-minute plenary discussion in which the organizers draw out from the whole group those matters which are seen to be important. These are best listed on a board or flipchart. It is not possible to say exactly what will emerge, but usually some or all of the following questions are raised:

1 Seating positions. Did people face each other or sit sideways on? How close did they sit?
2 Body posture. How were the participants sitting in their chairs? Was the interviewer leaning forward or away from the other person? Did both seem physically relaxed? If not what was the effect?
3 Body language. Did the physical postures or other mannerisms convey anything – interest, encouragement, anxiety, boredom and so on? Was there good eye contact throughout? Could anything be read from the interviewee's body language and facial expressions about their feelings and whether they were touching upon especially important matters.
4 Talking. Did the interviewee do the majority of the talking? How much time did the interviewer take and did he or she allow the other person to develop their own ideas or was there a tendency to intrude upon or redirect the line of thought? Could anything be derived from the tone of voice of both parties?
5 Questioning. What kinds of questions were used? Were they long or short? Did they encourage the interviewee to explore the subject in more depth? Could they be described as open or closed questions? This is a topic which is dealt with in more detail later but points which arise at this stage can usefully be noted for further reference.

The intention of the plenary is to help the participants to realize that there are many ways in which they can influence what happens in an interview – even without talking. It is important for interviewees to be encouraged to talk about matters that are important to them, and there are ways of achieving this, quite apart from the questions that are asked.

Questioning

Some points about different questioning styles might already have emerged from the earlier exercises, and it is now time to expand upon these. There are various ways of doing this but given the limited time available some fairly concise and structured information needs to be supplied. First, the difference between alternative types of question should be explained and the implications of using one type rather than another demonstrated. This can be done simply by asking participants to consider how they might react if the appraiser opened the interview with each of the following questions:

'How are things?'
'How are things at work?'
'How is your teaching going?'
'Have you any problems with your teaching?'
'Tell me about the problems you had with your teaching in the spring term?'
'What lay behind the difficulties you had with the third year in January?'
'When that problem blew up with the third year this term, would you put the cause down to one or two troublemakers or was it something you did or omitted to do?
'I think that your problem with the third year is the fact that you are too easy with them at the start of the year – what do you think?'

A list of questions of this kind can easily be constructed by the organizers to suit the nature of the group. It usually only takes five minutes to work through them, and the point being made comes across quickly and graphically. It is, however, useful to expand upon question styles still further, and a handout listing some of the more important categories of question can be prepared on the following lines.

Question types

The closed question

Normally used to elicit specific facts. Does not usually encourage elaboration by the interviewee. For example:

'When, exactly did that happen?'

'Who were the two boys involved?'
'Did you report it straight away?'

Probes

These are used to probe further into an answer. For instance, in relation to the three questions above, the following might be used to seek clarification or to expand upon the answer:

'What else was happening at the time?'
'Is there anything significant about these two boys being involved?'
'Why did you leave reporting the matter until the end of the day?'

Open questions

These are intended to allow interviewees to explore matters in their own way without feeling constrained by the nature of the question. For example:

'Will you tell me about the incident?'
'What do you think was going on?'
'I would appreciate your views on the next steps we should take?'

Reflective questions

These require the interviewee to reflect upon feelings and attitudes. The importance of this is picked up again later in connection with paraphrasing and summarizing. For example:

'You say you were not pleased when he said that?'
'How were you feeling after you had dealt with the matter?'
'Can you think back to the reasons that made you take that firm line?'

Leading questions

These place interviewees in a difficult situation: they must either follow the lead or challenge the question. They are generally not recommended. For instance:

'I assume that you did it that way because. . . . Is that right?'
'You were probably thinking about the consequences for the class as a whole when you did that – were you?'
'I think you had two choices open to you. . . . Surely it would have been sensible to have chosen the second one – wouldn't it?'

Multiple questions

Again these create difficulties for appraisees who have to remember all of the parts and decide which part to start with. They should be avoided whenever possible. One example will suffice:

'Tell me about the incident?' [This is a reasonable open question, but the interviewer continues.] 'What caused it? Why didn't you tell me immediately? Are you aware that it is my responsibility? What can we do to avoid it happening again? Do you realize that I will have to report it to the governors?'

There are various ways of proceeding after this document has been read and discussed by the participants – a task for which ten minutes should be allowed. One is for the organizers to prepare another sheet of mixed question types and ask individuals or pairs to categorize each one according to the 'question types' handout.

Another is to suggest a topic (e.g. my happiest time as a teacher or the best lesson I have ever given) for a five-minute practice interview using the trio format. Ask the interviewer to try to use only open or reflective questions and probes and the observer to pay particular attention to the questioning style. There is, however, another practice interview to come (in connection with paraphrasing and summarizing) and questioning styles can be built in as part of this activity thus saving some time.

Finally, if video-recording facilities are available, the organizers might like to prepare their own video demonstrating the various aspects of interviewing outlined above. This need not last more than ten minutes, and if carefully scripted can usefully demonstrate the different question types and their outcome. This can be particularly effective if, after several minutes of the interview, the same scene is re-enacted using, say, an open rather than a closed or leading question. Allow fifteen minutes for any of the above activities bringing the session, so far, to just over an hour.

Paraphrasing and summarizing

Paraphrasing and summarizing are key processes in interviewing for three reasons. First, the mere intention to practice them during an interview demands considerable concentration on the part of the appraiser. Second, they indicate to appraisees that they are being listened to very carefully. Third, they often invoke further elaboration by the appraisee and thus act as 'benign' probing questions.

Paraphrasing means repeating back to the interviewee the *essence* of what has just been said. This indicates that the message has been heard and understood and often acts as an encouragement to further reflection. The paraphrase should always be short – never long and rambling:

'Altogether it seems you were jolly frustrated.'

Or:

Interviewee: 'So if I apply for a job outside the area it means either a long journey every day or uprooting my family. If I don't make the effort to gain promotion I will continue to feel unhappy and frustrated where I am. I don't know which is best.'

Interviewer: 'It seems that whichever way you turn there are obstacles to be overcome.'

Summarizing means feeding back to the interviewee the *essence* of a longer piece, or possibly even the whole, of the interview. This requires attending skills of a high order. The summary should present the interviewee with his or her own views but in a more coherent, objective and integrated framework. The interviewer should have picked up recurring themes or problems and noted positive or negative attitudes or feelings associated with them. These will form the basis of the summary. For example, after part of an interview dealing with teaching over the past year, a summary might run as follows:

So far in our discussion you have raised a number of matters that have either caused you satisfaction or to think about your further development. You have gener-

ally felt pleased with your teaching and have been grati-
fied to hear from other teachers and parents that pupils
like your lessons and are well motivated in your subject.
Assessments of all kinds show that, overall, good progress is being made. But you have mentioned some areas
where you think that further improvements might be
made. You feel that you would like to become more
familiar with recent developments in approaches to
teaching in your subject and in particular to the more
creative use of computers. You are also not entirely
happy about how the new profiling system will affect
you. And finally there are a small number of pupils in
your class who are not progressing as well as you think
they should and you intend to raise this at the next
year-group meeting. Is that a fair summary? Would you
like to add any more before we move on?

These points about paraphrasing and summarizing should
be explained to participants either using an overhead projector
or handout. This should take about ten minutes. Another
short interview practice should then be arranged, wherever
possible allowing those who have not done so before to play
the role of interviewer. A handout suggesting the main skills
to be aware of should be made available to each trio to be read
out by one member of the group before the interview starts. It
might contain the following.

Interviewing skills: suggestions

1   Sit facing your partner and try to maintain good eye contact.
2   Be conscious of your own body posture, facial expression and tone of
    voice and try to encourage your partner to talk without interruption from
    you.
3   Watch your partner for signs of pleasure, anxiety or concern in facial
    expressions, body movement and changes of voice.
4   Use closed questions to establish specific facts but otherwise try to
    adopt an open-question approach supported by probes and reflective
    questions.
5   If possible do not rush in to fill silence with a question or response. It may

well be that your partner is thinking further about an issue and will be encouraged to say more by the space allowed.

6   Instead of replying directly to a point made by your partner try paraphrasing what has been said and note the response.

7   At the end of the interview summarize what has been said and ask for any further comments.

It is necessary to set up a simple interview task that will enable these skills to be practised. Normally, about fifteen minutes is needed and numerous possibilities exist. A counselling situation offers good scope for practising attending skills, and this can be made even more useful if an element of anxiety is built into the story that the interviewee has to relate. For instance:

Instructions for interviewee

You are a probationary teacher and you have recently taken over a class from a colleague who is away for an INSET term. There is one boy in the class who is causing you some problems. He is usually late, appears to be lazy and has more than once proved to be disruptive and a nuisance to others. You are suspicious that some insulting remarks that you found on the blackboard were written by him, but you have no proof. Also, although it may not be connected, a small group of boys (not from the school) who you think are his friends have twice followed you part of the way home calling out names and making threats. You decided today to tackle the problem face to face and asked him to stay behind. He did not do so and made, seemingly, insulting gestures at you as he ran off.

You are not sure what to do. If you go to the head, of whom you are somewhat in awe, you think that he might regard this as another case of your incompetence – following an incident when he felt he had to intervene to calm down one of your classes which he claimed was becoming overexcited. You therefore decide to call on the help of another colleague who you don't know very well but who appears to be a sympathetic sort of person. You meet in his classroom, which is now quiet after school, to discuss the matter.

Instructions to interviewer

You have been at the school for some years and know most of the teachers well. You are hoping soon that you will be promoted. You are also particularly interested in counselling.

A new teacher, still on probation, to whom you have chatted on a few occasions has asked to discuss a difficult problem with you after school. You don't know anything about the matter but can tell that it is something fairly serious and upsetting to the person concerned.

Bearing in mind the points made on the 'interviewing skills suggestions' sheet, find out as much as you can in fifteen minutes and try to help your colleague work out an appropriate solution without directions from you.

Instructions to observer

Here are the instructions given to the interviewer and interviewee. Using the points made on the 'interview suggestion' sheet, please observe the interview and note down all salient points for discussion afterwards.

Ten minutes should be allowed for the trios to discuss the exercise, followed by a plenary to hear the views of each group. To close the session the organizers should ask what people felt was the most significant thing learnt for them throughout the entire session and points made should be noted on a flipchart or blackboard. There will be some repetition of earlier comments, but this is not important as the intention is to reinforce some of the major problems that arise in interviewing and the skills that are necessary to overcome them. Overall, the entire session should take approximately one and three-quarter hours, although an extra ten minutes might reasonably be allowed for slippage.

Summary

This chapter deals with a workshop session intended to introduce participants to basic interviewing techniques associated with the skills of attending. These are listening and encouraging the other person to talk; questioning; and paraphrasing and summarizing. Because the session must be completed in under two hours, the aims are modest. They are to raise awareness of the key issues and skills which underlie effective interviewing and to equip the participants with sufficient knowledge and techniques to approach the main practice interview with confidence and the desire and ability to learn from the experience.

These aims are achieved by input from the organizers on the nature of the skills involved and by a series of short practice interviews, accompanied by observation and discussion, in which attending skills are practised.

Chapter 5

Interviewing skills II

This chapter deals with inputs and activities during the morning of the second day. These precede the main practice interviews in the afternoon and it is therefore worth reconsidering what has happened so far and what progress the participants should have made by this stage. This will give some indication as to what further ideas and help they will need before engaging in their interviews.

The group will at this point have considered the purposes of appraisal and have demonstrated for themselves that there is room for considerable divergence of view. They will also have become aware that people may hold a range of values and that these will affect the principles which form the basis for systems and schemes of appraisal. Hopefully, they will also have realized that they are dealing with a controversial matter and that there is the possibility of genuine uncertainty and misunderstanding about what appraisal could or should be able to achieve.

But in order to move forward and to carry out effective interviews, group members need to have a framework upon which to base their approach. For this purpose, a joint problem-solving model (as described in Ch. 3) was suggested. This should enable participants to be clear about their respective roles as appraisers and appraisees.

Next, they will have dealt with the basic interviewing skills of listening, questioning and summarizing and have practised some of these in mini-interviews. These are necessary as 'ice-breakers' prior to the main interviews and also to demons-trate that so-called attending skills are necessary in order to conduct an effective interview.

There are, however, numerous questions still outstanding, and the entire morning is devoted to further preparation in areas which participants should, themselves, help to identify. Typical questions which may arise are:

1 What format should the interview take? Is there a normal procedure that should be followed?
2 How should I conduct the interview making sure that I keep in control and cover all the ground?
3 How should I tackle difficult issues which might involve some criticism of the appraisee?
4 What happens at the end of the interview with regard to target setting?

These questions are all important and it is necessary to deal with them carefully in order to raise the confidence and skills of the prospective interviewers. There are many ways in which this might be done, and as a result this session has in the past tended to be one of the most flexible and experimental parts of the workshop. The method suggested here begins with group work in which members seek to identify their own problems, followed by a search for solutions using training videos of one kind or another.

Controlling the interview

The appraisal interview is not like a counselling session, although counselling skills may be useful or necessary at times as demonstrated in Chapter 4. Certain types of counselling are sometimes described as 'client-centred or client-directed'. In this situation the interviewer responds to the perceived needs of the client as they emerge. The counsellor remains in control but takes directional cues from the client. There are generally times in an appraisal interview when this will happen, but over and above this the appraiser must take responsibility for keeping to an agenda and moving the process forward to reach a positive ending involving plans for the future. What are the skills necessary to achieve this?

Group task

In groups of four. Two members of the group are asked, in turn, to imagine that they are to hold their first appraisal interview next week with a member of staff who has the following characteristics:

is respected as a good teacher;
holds strong political views;
has, from time to time, been critical of management for being indecisive or
    weak;
is not afraid to voice opinions.

They should tell the group what problems they think might arise for them in the interview situation. After they have expressed their thoughts and feelings the group should attempt to suggest ways in which these problems might be overcome or alleviated. The time allowed for this is twenty minutes.

The other two members of the group are then asked to consider their likely problems in connection with a member of staff who is:

young, inexperienced, generally thought of as an adequate teacher but with
    much to learn;
generally very quiet and unforthcoming in discussions;
seems to lack confidence;
is something of a loner in the school and seldom stays behind after hours.

Again, the same process should be followed and the discussion completed in twenty minutes.

This forty-minute exercise should be followed by a thirty-minute plenary session to hear what problems are predicted, whether the same problems exist irrespective of the characteristics of the interviewee and what steps might be taken to deal with the problems.

It is useful if one of the organizers makes a list on a flipchart or blackboard showing the problems and possible solutions. It is impossible to say with any degree of certainty what might arise, and it is important not to let the group dwell for too long on any one issue. It is also important to emphasize solutions and ways of avoiding problems. Participants should be asked to record for themselves both problems and solutions and to consider them against the video to be shown in the next session.

Here are some examples of problems that might occur to participants and some possible solutions they might put forward.

1   How to put the appraisee at ease.
    Possible solution: Draw up an agenda beforehand so that they have some say in the matter and know what areas will be covered. Ensure privacy and set a definite time limit. Provide comfortable, face-to-face seating. Explain procedures and what will happen at the end regarding target setting and reporting. Deal with areas of satisfaction first and give genuine praise where it is deserved.
2   What to do when there is silence.
    Possible action: Allow it to continue for longer than you normally would. (Most people find even the shortest break in conversation difficult to handle.) Ask if the appraisee has any more to say on the subject or if you can assume that silence means agreement. Alternatively, try paraphrasing the last statement or summarizing the discussion so far and see if this brings a response. Otherwise move on.
3   How best to stop somebody talking without creating tension in the discussion.
    Possible strategies: Remind them of the agenda and the time. Suggest that the matter is one that might be dealt with separately outside of the appraisal interview. Ask for a written report on the subject. If necessary, interrupt and move on to the next item.

These are not necessarily the best, the correct or the only solutions to such common problems, but they alert participants to difficult areas and provide good preparation for viewing the video tapes. Other problems which are often mentioned are:

How to give praise without sounding patronizing.
The best way to introduce what might be a sensitive area.
Handling criticism – expressed or implied – of oneself.
Moving on and pacing.
Probing for further information.
Saying things that might be disappointing to the interviewee.
Saying no.
And so on.

The session should be brought to a close after an hour and a half and then up to thirty minutes allowed for a break and informal discussion.

Video presentation and discussion

An hour and three-quarters is scheduled for this session of which the last half-hour should be devoted to a consideration of target-setting and reporting.

It is important that participants have the opportunity to see and discuss an interview in order to relate the problems identified earlier to the actual face to face process of an appraisal interview. Videos are useful in this respect, and an hour and a quarter is allowed for viewing and discussion.

No single film is ideal for this purpose despite the fact that a number of training films have been specially made and marketed. Those available at present can all be criticized for being either too bland, too hard-edged, not applicable to education, too humorous, too patronizing and so on. Even if organizers are fortunate enough to be able to make their own film of a real interview and obtain permission to use it for training purposes, people will still find plenty of things to criticize in it.

But criticism is not a problem in this context. Good points or bad points identified by participants can all be used to illustrate what is happening in the interview and what is likely to be helpful or harmful in the process. For this reason it does not matter too much which film is used, but some mention is made of a few possibilities.

How Am I Doing, featuring John Cleese (Video Arts 1983) is, as might be imagined, a funny but insightful film and is primarily intended for industrial training. It raises many of the crucial issues concerning appraisal interviewing generally and makes the points cogently through the clever use of humour. If participants raise the point that it applies to industry and not education a fruitful discussion can often be encouraged by asking what the differences are as they apply to the appraisal process?

The Appraisal Interview (Cambridgeshire County Council 1984) is based upon an annual appraisal of an LEA officer by a senior official. The issues under review are mainly concerned with educational planning at county level, but there is a probing performance review culminating in a discussion of the appraisee's career plans, prospects and development needs.

The interview is often regarded by participants as a 'hard-edged' approach and many shy away from the penetrating questioning style and attempts to quantify performance outcomes. As a video for raising points and demonstrating various techniques, however, it is extremely useful and can be relied upon to cause heated discussion – even if the conclusion for some is 'that is not how I would want to do it'.

Understanding the Appraisal Interview features the director of a research project on appraisal in the ILEA (Trotman 1986). This is one of a series of films on teacher appraisal, all of which are useful for different purposes. This one shows extracts from three role-play interviews: two with teachers in primary schools and one with a teacher in a secondary school. The interviewer plays the part of the head and has clearly visited the appraisees in their school and knows something of their situation. They all discuss their own work as they would in a real interview. The importance of this video is that it demonstrates very clearly the possible structure of an interview moving through a sequence of steps: opening, giving positive feedback, dealing with areas of concern, discussing development needs and career aspirations and finally summarizing and target setting.

It generally invokes two reactions from participants. Some

find it reassuring and feel that if that is what appraisal is all about then there should be no problems. They suggest that they would be happy to follow this approach and feel that staff would accept it. The other view is that it does not probe deeply enough nor challenge the appraisee. Some feel it to be too bland and, in parts, patronizing. But despite these criticisms the film is helpful in building confidence and illustrating the sequential steps that those unused to the process might follow, at least, initially.

Appraisal Skills (Gower 1987) is again based upon an interview in an industrial setting and is directed by management consultants specializing in appraisal training. It uses experienced actors and is a sophisticated production. It brings out many of the major problems inherent in all appraisal interviewing and demonstrates the nature, purpose and phases of an interview very well. It uses a 'replay' technique most effectively by showing a sequence and then returning to the beginning in order to analyse what went wrong. The sequence is then shown again with the interviewer using a different approach.

Again participants usually have different views about the interview. It clearly shows an authority structure not normally found in schools. The questioning is far from bland and some people find this unacceptable. On the other hand, it demonstrates well the use of a joint problem-solving technique which involves the employee in identifying and seeking solutions to matters of common concern. Whatever views are held by the group, it is a film that will invoke discussion about key issues and techniques used in appraisal.

Other new materials There is little doubt that more training materials will appear over the coming years. Already most of the pilot LEAs are engaged in the process of making videotapes or training packages. Newcastle upon Tyne LEA hope to release their materials in September 1988 (Newcastle LEA 1988). Suffolk LEA has a package of 3 tapes already available (Suffolk LEA 1988). The National Development Centre has produced a bibliography on Appraisal and a supplement contains 4 pages of audio visual material now available (NDC 1988).

The use of published and other materials

The cost of videos varies considerably from about £70 in the case of the Cambridgeshire film to £650 for the Gower *Appraisal Skills*, although some can be hired for short periods.

An alternative is for organizers to make their own film. The SFSD project team made various attempts to do this and with varying degrees of success. Here are some of the problems to be overcome. They are not insuperable but they do need careful consideration, time and patience.

1   Location. If a studio is available this will generally offer the best facilities in the way of equipment, lighting and so on. Otherwise, it is essential to have a quiet private room with good lighting. A trial run for a few minutes is a good policy.

2   Role-play or real? It is possible to create a situation which offers sufficient information for the two parties to play the role of appraiser and appraisee. For instance, the case study in Appendix II provided the SFSD team with a number of interviews which were videotaped and later used in workshops. But generally it is better to come closer to reality and film two people in a real interview situation.

3   Who will take part? It is best to have people who feel reasonably confident in the roles of appraiser and appraisee and preferably two who have experienced the interview situation together on previous occasions. Ideally they should follow an interview structure which is close to the one recommended for workshop participants. This helps to establish the stages prior to the practice interview.

4   Permission. Agreement must be obtained for the film to be used for training purposes. The actors must be made aware that however good they may think their performance, it will, inevitably, be criticized by those with inadequate knowledge of the situation or with different views about the nature and purpose of the appraisal. How the actors should be rewarded for their involvement and their permission to use the film is one that clearly needs to be considered.

Videotapes, whether commercial or home-made, will vary in length but generally they will run for between thirty minutes and an hour. On the commercial tapes there are usually introductions and conclusions which can sometimes be dispensed with, and once the organizers know the script well, it is possible to skip parts that are repetitious or refer to matters already dealt with in earlier workshop sessions. An ideal showing time seems to be about thirty to forty minutes. After this, concentration generally flags and there is a danger of boredom.

Half an hour, at least, is necessary for discussion after showing a video film, and this should, as far as possible, be directed towards the problems identified earlier rather than the quality of the film.

To sum up, it does not matter too much about the quality of the interview shown on the film, provided it illustrates some of the issues and problems mentioned above and sufficient time is allowed for discussion. The audio-visual portrayal of a (more or less) complete interview is important for participants who until this point have dealt with only separate aspects of the appraisal interview. Perhaps for the first time they are able to gain some sense of 'what it will be like'.

Targets

Trethowan (1987), in his book *Appraisal and Target Setting*, places targets at the heart of the appraisal process, and his comments are helpful in offering guidance to workshop participants. He provides some guidelines about forming effective targets as follows:

1   Express them as end results not as processes or activities.
2   Make them as definite as possible and avoid ambiguity.
3   Agree them to be achievable within a stated time period.
4   Make them practical and feasible, not theoretical and idealistic.
5   Select only those which are important and of real consequence to the job.

6 Make them precise, not too indefinite nor too complex.
7 Set a limit of one important target in each statement; avoid having several targets combined into one.
8 Aim to stretch the target holder, personally and professionally.
9 Allow opportunity for redefining targets if circumstances change.
10 Tailor the targets to suit the person, relating them to the teacher's career where possible.
11 Do not exceed six targets for a teacher; between four and six is ideal.
12 State the criteria for success.
13 Agree them to be realistic, noting underachievers (who set their targets too low) and overachievers (who are aiming too high).
14 Aim to make your staff realistic achievers, who set high but attainable targets.

(Trethowan 1987:44)

These criteria can be displayed on a board, flipchart or transparency and examples of one or two targets shown alongside. For example, any of the following might be used for discussion purposes:

1 To teach French successfully to Set 3D and judge success on the basis of (a) the results of the French GOALS examination, (b) the number of pupils from 3D selecting French or French studies for their fourth-year course, (c) the view of the pupils as judged by the teacher (ibid.: 41).
2 To establish a tighter system of control over the purchase and use of laboratory equipment in the upper school. The new system to be in place, and understood by all staff involved, ready for the autumn term. The cost of the new scheme not to exceed £300.
3 To attend the six sessions on profiling (or language development or special needs etc.) provided by the county next term and to prepare for the school a draft policy on this issue for discussion by all staff on the INSET day

agreed for December. A preliminary draft to be discussed with the head before the end of November.

Participants should be asked to consider whether these meet the first seven criteria for targets as set out above. The remaining seven are difficult to apply without knowing the individual for whom they are set. There should then be a small exercise to reinforce the above points.

Targets

In pairs, write a target which satisfies as many of the above criteria as possible. You have ten minutes.

After this brief initiation into the art of target setting, participants should be reminded of the fact that their practice interviews should end with a set of agreed and written targets. The last interviewer in the practice interviews (see p. 65) must be prepared for this and allow time accordingly. Realistically, for an exercise of this nature, no more than four targets will be expected and generally the number produced is either two or three.

This completes the preparation for the afternoon sessions. The interviews will undoubtedly raise points for clarification and further matters and it is, therefore, important to allow at least half an hour for a plenary at the end as described in chapter six.

Summary

This chapter deals with input and preparation prior to the practice interviews. It covers the problem of structuring and controlling interviews and encourages participants to identify and suggest solutions to their own problems. Use is then made of a videotape of an interview to allow members to obtain a view of 'what it is like'. Subsequent discussion is aimed at linking the participants' own problems and solutions with the situation portrayed in the film. Some aspects of commercial or 'home-made videos and their use are dealt with. Finally, target setting is considered and members are given some practice in writing these.

Chapter 6

The practice interview

We now come to the final part of the workshop which brings together all of the previous inputs, discussions and practice. The participants will soon engage in what, for many, will feel like a real appraisal interview, and there is generally an air of anticipation and excitement about the whole exercise. It is therefore important that those involved should be provided with facilities that they would normally require in the real situation, particularly a quiet, private room and comfortable seating.

The practice groups

Two people can learn a great deal by interviewing each other in turn and discussing their reactions afterwards. But because they are involved in the actual task of interviewing or being interviewed, they are likely to miss a great many important aspects of their own words, actions and reactions. This could be partly overcome by the use of a video-recorder, which would permit a review of the process followed by discussion and feedback – possibly involving other workshop participants as well. But there are several drawbacks to using video equipment. First, it requires those concerned to be aware of something happening outside of the interview, and this can be distracting. Second, the rerun of the tape takes at least the time of the interview – usually an hour – and discussion of points as they arise, possibly accompanied by further reruns, can take several hours altogether. With limited time this is simply not possible. Third, a video-camera would be necessary for each group, and unless the whole training group is very small this is normally not possible.

In order to overcome the observation problem, the following experimental format, which has now been used on numerous occasions, is recommended.

> *Participants form groups of four, one of whom is interviewed. The other three take it in turn to cover part of the interview. At any one time there are, therefore, always two observers.*

This arrangement lies at the heart of the whole interview training approach adopted in this book. Everything else that has been suggested so far relates to and supports this particular interviewing format. There are clearly a number of questions raised by the method described above, and answers to these only began to emerge with any degree of certainty after several workshops had been organized along similar lines. What follows, therefore, is an explanation of the method adopting what seem to be the most appropriate answers to these questions.

1 How is the appraisee chosen?

Each group of four is asked to decide upon the appraisee between themselves. On no occasion has there been any difficulty. At least one person usually volunteers, and if there is more than one the participants find their own criteria for choosing which person to select.

2 Do the interviewers have sufficient information?

The volunteer is required to give a copy of the completed pro-forma to the three other members of the group and then to withdraw. The three interviewers then have thirty minutes to read the form, discuss their approach and decide what further factual information they require from the interviewee. If additional facts are needed, these are normally sought at the beginning of the interview or, preferably, in a ten-minute agenda setting and information-seeking session prior to the main interview. It is generally found that the information obtained via the pro-forma and through some brief introductory questions is more than adequate for the interview.

3   *What do appraisees do whilst waiting for the interviewers to read and discuss the pro-formas?*

The appraisees (five, if the workshop is organized for twenty participants) can be brought together as a group for discussion. It has been found valuable to ask them to write down, singly and then as a group, what they would expect to feel at the end of a real and well-conducted appraisal interview. Their responses can be written out on a flipchart and used in the final plenary session as part of a discussion of the benefits of a 'good' appraisal.

4   *How can the interview be divided into three separate parts without appearing stilted and unreal?*

This is perhaps one of the most important issues raised by this method. If it is to work there should be a 'natural' structure to the interview, but this is a controversial point. Some would argue that the nature of the interview and the interviewing style adopted will depend upon a number of factors, including the personality of the appraiser, his or her relationship with the appraisee and the particular context in which the interview takes place. To suggest a set format is therefore artificial and inhibiting. But against this it has to be remembered that for many people this is their first experience of appraisal interviewing. Most are looking for a way forward, a method of practising which will enable them to build up confidence and develop their own style and approach. A set format for the interview at this stage is therefore a useful 'crutch' but one that can be discarded at a later stage as expertise begins to develop. Again, using the golf analogy, it is like the standard grip and swing that a professional will demonstrate to a novice. Once the basics are learnt these will be adapted to fit with physical characteristics such as height, length of arms and so on, and to an inherent sense of timing thought to be associated with personality factors.

A possible structure for appraisal interviews is suggested by John Yates and demonstrated in the video referred to in

Chapter 5 (Trotman 1986). This suggests a series of steps through which the interview should progress and for the purpose of the present workshop these can be grouped into three phases as follows:

Phase 1: Welcoming interviewee and putting at ease, explaining the purpose of the interview, asking for information or clarifying factual matters and finally dealing with areas of satisfaction over the past year which can be praised.

Phase 2: Dealing with areas that the appraisee has indicated (through the pro-forma responses) have proved to be less than satisfactory or to have been the cause of some concern.

Phase 3: Considering career aspirations, ideas for further education, training and development, setting targets for the coming year and bringing the interview to a close.

These three phases appear to follow a logical order and to offer a sound structure for the practice interview. A different interviewer conducts each phase. Feedback from workshop participants in the past has generally supported the format outlined above provided it is seen as a way of learning interviewing techniques and not as a hard-and-fast set of rules to be followed on all occasions. Normally, the three sections will take about equal time (roughly fifteen to twenty minutes each) but there is tendency to concentrate more on phase 2 in practice interviews – a point worthy of discussion in later, plenary sessions.

5   *What happens at the end of each phase?*
There are two alternatives at the end of a phase; either the second interviewer can 'take the chair' and carry straight on or there can be a deliberate break for discussion. It is claimed by some that the former provides a smoother and more natural interview, but those that have tried both methods argue that the break and discussion between each phase offers a far greater learning opportunity.

There are a number of points in its favour. The two observers have the opportunity to raise points shortly after they have happened and whilst they are still fresh in the minds of the participants, rather than at the end of an hour. They can obtain information from the interviewer and interviewee about their thoughts and feelings on the way the interview is proceeding and they can give feedback on their perceptions as to what is going well and what may be going wrong. The second interviewer is therefore able to gain from the discussion important clues as to how to proceed. The break after the second phase provides similar possibilities plus the opportunity to re-examine some of the points made in the first break and to consider how far they were taken into account in phase two. The final discussion, as well as considering phase 3, can examine the experience of the interview as a whole. The time which is allowed for the interview itself and accompanying discussion should normally be about an hour and three-quarters. Any less time than this tends to frustrate important discussion.

6   *Can the observers be relied upon to give helpful feedback?*
In the sessions which precede the practice interviews, matters such as listening skills, questioning styles and constructive feedback have been discussed. Participants are encouraged to be alert to the use of these skills both in the interviews which they will observe and also in their own feedback sessions with the interviewer and interviewee. The use of special forms which provide a structured format for observation was considered and tried on a few occasions. Generally the feedback from those who used them was that they were found to be distracting and confusing and not at all helpful. On the whole they preferred to use a notebook and learn what to look for from experience. Structured forms may, however, be more appropriate in advanced training workshops.

7   *What happens to the appraisee's pro-forma?*
Pro-formas are returned to the interviewee at the end of the interview so that there is no problem about confidentiality.

8   *Does everyone have a chance to practise interviewing?*
If only one interview takes place, then three people share the interviewing experience and only one person is interviewed.

In a short workshop this may be all that is possible unless some of the other activities referred to in earlier chapters are curtailed or abandoned. As already pointed out, it is important to provide the opportunity for a full discussion about the nature and purpose of appraisal and the skills which are appropriate to good interviewing before the practice interview takes place and any reduction in the time allocated to these sessions must be carefully considered. Participants involved in the workshops organized to date have generally not complained about being restricted to the role of either interviewer or interviewee. Both roles appear to offer good insights into the appraisal process.

However, if time can be found either by extending the length of the workshop day or having an extra day, it should be possible to offer a second practice interview, using a different appraisee. This will ensure that everyone has some practice at interviewing. This decision is one that can only be made by workshop organizers.

Follow-up plenary

It is important to allow at least an hour after the practice interviews for those involved to discuss their experiences. The chairperson will normally seek responses from each group of four and encourage others to compare and contrast their own views.

It is also useful at this stage to refer back to the discussion held with the appraisees before their interview and to ask how far their expectations of an 'ideal' interview compared with what actually happened. If these have been written on a flipchart they can be considered point by point. Appraisers are often surprised both by the list of criteria drawn up by the appraisees and also how many of these have been achieved, even in a practice interview.

Finally, some attention might be given to further steps that appraisees might take to build upon their experience and to improve the skills learnt so far. Some possibilities are considered in Chapter 7.

Evaluation

The kind of evaluation that is done must be left to organizers to decide, but certainly some form of feedback should be obtained, usually to satisfy the requirements of the LEA concerned but more importantly in order to obtain information for revising and modifying future workshops as necessary.

A simple questionnaire is recommended either to be completed before participants leave or a few days later. If completed on the premises, there should be a high rate of return of forms, whereas this may be considerably reduced if they are taken away to be returned later. Against this, however, it can be argued that people need a little time to absorb the experience and to be less rushed in giving their views. The relative advantages and disadvantages of the timing must therefore be considered by the organizers.

A questionnaire might contain some or all of the following questions.

1 Were you sufficiently informed about and prepared for the workshop?
2 To what extent were your expectations met?
3 What were the main strengths of the workshop?
4 What were its weaknesses?
5 What particular activities did you find useful?
6 Which activities were less useful?
7 Was the order and pacing of activities about right?
8 What changes would you recommend if the workshop were to be repeated?
9 Will you be engaging in follow-up activities? If so please say what you will be doing?
10 How would you now feel if asked to engage in a real appraisal interview?

There are many more questions which might be included and organizers are recommended to spend some time on preparing the form according to their own need for information. Ideally it would be valuable to have follow-up interviews with some participants to obtain reactions a few weeks later, but clearly this will depend upon the time available.

The method summarized

Before the workshop each participant is sent a pro-forma on the lines described in Chapter 2 and asked to complete it and bring three extra copies to the workshop. After introductory sessions dealing with the nature and purpose of appraisal, the skills necessary and the structure of the practice interview, participants are placed in groups of four. Each group decides upon one person to be interviewed, and this person hands copies of the completed pro-forma to the other three members of the group. These three then take forty-five minutes to read the pro-forma, discuss it and decide upon their approach to the interview. They may decide to talk briefly to the appraisee before the interview in order to obtain any extra information they require. The appraisee will also join those from the other groups to discuss what they would ideally like to receive from a good interview.

When the interviews take place (all in separate rooms) each of the three appraisers will take it in turn to carry out a part of the interview. For this purpose the interview is divided into three phases. The first deals with introductions, explanations and parts of the job which have given the appraisee satisfaction. The second deals with areas which have given less satisfaction or which have provided grounds for concern. The final part considers career aspirations, staff development needs and targets for the coming year.

A discussion takes place after each part during which time points can be raised by the interviewer, the interviewee or the observers.

The pro-formas are handed back to the appraisees at the end of the session. The interview and discussion will normally take two hours. The whole process can be repeated, if time is available, using a different appraisee.

The practice interview is followed immediately by a plenary session during which the learning which has occurred is discussed together with further steps which participants might take to enhance their learning. Finally, the workshop is evaluated and in this chapter some key questions are suggested.

Chapter 7

Further action

Is two days enough to engage with the obvious complexities of appraisal training? The approach described in the previous chapters was deliberately restricted in this way because, for most workshops organized to date, this was all the time that was available. Furthermore, it seems unlikely that, given the extent of the training task which will face local education authorities in the future, much more time will ever be allowed – this, despite the strong recommendation in the Suffolk report (Graham 1987) that structured training should take a *minimum* of three consecutive days.

In two days, quite a lot can be achieved, but ideally more time is necessary, and in this chapter two possibilities are considered: first, some uses of additional workshop time, assuming this was made available, and second, further action which might be taken by participants after a two day workshop.

An extra day

An additional day would make a considerable difference to the way a workshop of the kind described earlier is organized, and below are some of the possibilities as to how the extra time might be used to good effect. It is difficult to suggest priorities because much will depend upon the kind of group involved and the ideas and assumptions which underpin the proposed appraisal scheme for which the workshop is organized. The list below should therefore be regarded as a menu from which to select items. Also, depending upon circumstances and the organizer's preference, some of these ideas might be used to replace those included in the two-day model already described.

Additional practice interviewing time

Although there have been no complaints about the fact that one person (the appraisee) does not have the opportunity to interview, there seems little doubt that an extra round of interviewing would be beneficial. It would allow everyone to engage in at least one phase of the process; it would mean that three out of four people would have the opportunity to interview in two different phases, and finally, it would offer immediate reinforcement of the learning which took place in the first round. The extra one and three-quarter hours necessary for this would be time well spent.

Appraisal schemes

Although some time was allowed on the first day to consider the principles which might underlie a scheme of appraisal, this was left as uncompleted business, and a general (joint problem-solving model) was suggested in order to provide participants with a set of guidelines upon which to base their practice interviews. But the design of an appraisal scheme for a school requires much more detail than this, and many questions were left unanswered.

Participants might be asked, in company with others from the same or a similar school to produce an appraisal policy covering some or all of the following matters.

(i) General

To what extent will staff be consulted and involved in drawing up the scheme?

How will this process take place?
Will involvement in whatever scheme is produced be voluntary or compulsory?

(ii) Pre-interview

What preparation should there be by:
the appraiser,
the appraisee,
others?

Upon what aspects of a teachers work should pre-interview preparation concentrate? What information should become available as a result? How should it be used?

(iii) Interview

Who will interview?
Might more than one person be involved?
Will appraisees have any choice in this?
When will it take place?
How often?
How much time will be allowed?
Will a prior agenda be set?
How will the purposes be agreed and communicated?
What approach/style will be adopted?
What will be the main elements of the interview?
Will targets be set?
Who will set them?

(iv) Post interview

Will a report be produced?
By whom?
What will it contain?
Is it necessary that it should be agreed and signed by both parties?
Will it remain confidential to both parties?
If not, who else may see it?
For what purposes will it be used?

What action will flow from the interview?
Who will be responsible for monitoring progress?

Will an appeals procedure be necessary?
Why?

What kind is appropriate?

(v) Other matters considered important

Appraisal involves many complex issues and the above list is far from comprehensive. Section (v) therefore allows for further matters to be recorded as they arise in discussion. The exercise, preferably in groups of at least six, needs one and a half to two hours plus an extra half an hour in plenary to hear and discuss the problems that have arisen. Groups could be provided with background reading (perhaps overnight, after the second day) and might include, for instance, the ACAS report (ACAS 1986) or extracts from other documents suggesting ideas for schemes such as the Suffolk reports (Graham 1985, 1987).

Evidence for appraisal

What kind of evidence is appropriate or necessary for an appraisal interview and how should it be obtained? These are questions which, in a two-day workshop, receive only scant attention. They are, nevertheless, important matters because the answers will largely determine the design of the appraisal scheme.

The teacher's job involves many roles and activities, and these can be divided into a number of main areas. The ACAS report (ACAS 1986), for instance, suggests planning and preparation, classroom organization and management, teaching skills, relationships and general responsibilities such as administration, attention to care and safety and so on. All of these can be further subdivided into specific tasks or responsibilities. The ACAS document lists between thirty and forty, depending upon the different teacher grades.

Most teachers will challenge some of the items on the list and will wish to add others. A useful exercise can be built around this aspect of job analysis and, at the same time, linked to the problem of evidence.

   (i)   In sub-groups consider the ACAS list or roles and tasks (or any other list which may be available) and modify it as seems appropriate.

(ii)   Consider each item and suggest evidence which might be appropriate to help determine performance in each category. For instance, if the agreed statements included:

'maintains an effective working environment' or

'shows consideration for both teaching and non-teaching colleagues'

then what evidence would be needed to verify these and how would it be obtained?

Time allowed: one and a half hours.

Classroom observation

The need for classroom observation as a means of obtaining evidence is almost certain to emerge from the preceding exercise. Although it was stated in Chapter 1 that this book would not deal in detail with this matter, it is difficult to discuss appraisal training without some mention of the subject.

One reason for not including classroom observation in a two–day workshop is the time factor. It is a complex area and it deserves a workshop of its own. But if an extra day is allowed, then its inclusion should at least be considered. It is strongly argued by some that appraisal cannot or should not take place unless it is based upon first-hand knowledge by the appraiser of the appraisee's main task – classroom teaching. The ACAS document (ACAS 1986) states that classroom observation 'will be an essential feature of appraisal, but the purposes and objectives are still to be fully investigated in the pilot projects'.

Wragg (1987) has produced 'a practical guide' for teacher appraisal and this concentrates upon classroom observation as the central part of an appraisal scheme. He also suggests a useful exercise which could be incorporated into an appraisal training workshop. This is summarized on the facing page.

Classroom observation: what do we look for? (Summarized from Wragg 1987.)

Purpose: To devise what features of lessons might be most worthy of analysis and discussion with the teacher concerned. Allow 60 to 120 minutes.

Required: A videotape (20–30 minutes) of a lesson as similar as possible to what is typical for the group concerned.

Step 1: The group should watch the video imagining that an interview is to be held with the teacher afterwards. Each person should make notes during the video about what aspects of the lesson might be discussed.

Steps 2 and 3: In subgroups individuals compare notes, discuss findings and agree key headings for observation.

Steps 4 and 5: Sub groups draw up pro-formas for making notes that might be used by observers for the purpose of a subsequent appraisal. The pro-formas are photocopied and compared.

Wragg's book will be useful to organizers wishing to introduce classroom observation skills into an appraisal workshop. The following are also helpful: Walker and Adeleman (1975), Stubbs and Delamont (1976), Boehm and Weinberg (1977) (see References).

Before leaving the subject it is worth raising a few points of caution which offer a view running counter to the general acceptance of classroom observation as a central part of appraisal schemes.

1 The skills involved in classroom observation are considerable, and if it is to be carried out sensitively and effectively, specific training will be necessary. It is doubtful whether simply tacking it on to an appraisal workshop will be sufficient on its own.

2 Appraisal can, in any case, be done without classroom observation. The practice interviews which workshop participants carry out using only a self-evaluation form bear witness to this fact.

3   Classroom observation can be an important part of teacher development, but need it be linked to appraisal? If it is separated from the process then it may be more likely to open the way to self-appraisal or peer appraisal through mutual classroom observation. See, for instance, Elliot-Kemp and Rogers (1982), Elliot-Kemp (1986), Rudduck (1982).

4   A different but important point concerns the cost of appraisal. If each appraisal involves time for classroom observation (and some might suggest that more than one observation is necessary in order to be fair), then the overall time needed for each appraisal is likely to amount to ten or more hours. Can this time be found for every teacher in every school? Will the government or LEAs be prepared to finance such a costly venture?

These points are not intended to downgrade the value of classroom observation, especially if it is properly carried out by those experienced in the various techniques, but rather to raise the issue of its importance, or otherwise, as part of an appraisal system.

Post-workshop activities

At the end of workshops, although participants might feel enthusiastic about the experience and what they have learnt, there is the inevitable return to the everyday problems of school life and pressures which, despite the best of intentions, may lessen the impact of training. This can be overcome to some extent by encouraging post-workshop activities. Below are some ideas which are drawn from the action taken by participants in previous workshops.

1   Each member draws up an action plan during the course of the workshop specifying targets and means of monitoring their achievement. If organizers intend that this should be done, then time will have to be found at the end, possibly by extending the workshop for a further hour. To add motivation to the exercise it is suggested that members

work in pairs and agree to check with each other that targets have been achieved.

2 Create networks of people who will continue to meet to discuss matters of common concern, engage in further practice or work together producing reports, materials, policy statements and so on.

3 More specifically, such groups might:

(a) continue practice interviews amongst themselves using pro-formas, as in the workshop;

(b) observe each other teaching and use the information obtained from this activity to enhance the practice interviews.

(c) design self-evaluation pro-formas specifically for use within their own school(s);

(d) produce videotapes of appraisal interviews;

(e) hold interviews with members of staff in their own school(s) on a voluntary basis and use the group as a sounding board to discuss progress and problems;

(f) consider the problem of appraising the 'poor performer' and whether interviews with teachers who fall into this category require special approaches or techniques;

(g) help each other with drawing up appraisal schemes for specific schools;

(h) write a position paper for the LEA on appraisal or appraisal training;

(i) plan further appraisal training workshops;

(j) visit other areas or schools to discuss different approaches to appraisal;

(k) evaluate appraisal materials such as books, practical guides, videotapes and so on.

Local education authorities will, hopefully, wish to encourage this kind of activity and provide some extra resources to enable it to take place. It should certainly be regarded as an important form of follow-up which will help to ensure that the value of the workshop itself is not lost in the normal pressures of everyday life.

Summary

In this, the final chapter, the possibility of further action is considered on the basis of either an extra workshop day or post-workshop activities by participants. In the case of the former it was suggested that the additional time might be most profitably used for: further practice interviews, drawing up a detailed appraisal scheme for a school or for some training in classroom observation. The need for classroom observation as part of appraisal, however, was questioned.

Post-workshop activities, preferably related to individual or group action plans, might include, for instance, practice interviews within a group, similar to those carried out during the workshop; mutual classroom observation, interviews with members of staff and reporting back to the group; an investigation of any special problems which might arise in connection with interviewing those teachers regarded as poor performers; production of self-evaluation pro-formas; making of videotapes of appraisal interviews; drawing up schemes of appraisal for individual schools, visits to other schools to learn about alternative approaches to appraisal; writing a position paper; evaluating training materials. The hope was expressed that LEAs would regard post-workshop action as an integral part of appraisal training and make available some small additional resources by way of encouragement.

Appendix I

The programme: a two-day workshop on appraisal interviewing for teachers

Day one

9.00 am	Arrive and register.
9.30 am	Introduction and explanation of mode of working (see Ch. 3).
9.45 am	The purposes and context of appraisal (see Ch. 3).
11.00 am	Break.
11.15 am	Key issues in appraisal and their effect upon the interview (see Ch. 3).
12.45 pm	Break for lunch.
2.00 pm	Interviewing skills: listening, questioning and summarizing (see Ch. 4).
3.30 pm	Break.
3.45 pm	Interviewing skills continued (see Ch. 4).
5.15 pm	Close.

Day two

9.00 am	Interviewing skills: control, target-setting and reporting (see Ch. 5).
11.00 am	Break.

11.15 am	Structure of interview: video and discussion (see Ch. 5).
12.45 pm	Lunch.
2.00 pm	Preparing for interview (see Ch. 6).
2.30 pm	Practice interviews (see Ch. 6).
4.15 pm	Break.
4.30 pm	Final plenary (see Ch. 6).
5.30 pm	Close.

Appendix II

Primary school case study: an appraisal role-play scenario

Eric Hewton and Tony Ward

This material, prepared for the East Sussex School-Focused Staff Development Project 1986, provides background information for an appraisal interview for Chris Unwin (deputy head) by Pat Lasalle (the head). An organization chart relevant to the interview is appended. It is current (though recent) practice to hold one formal interview each year.

Other figures to appear in the study are:

Ms Llewellin   i/c Art and music
Ms James   i/c Science
Mr Doberman   a parent

You will be playing the role of appraiser and/or appraisee or observer. Appraisers and appraisee will receive a different set of papers which deal with similar matters from slightly different perspectives. Observers will receive all of these papers.

Your task is to prepare for the interview in the circumstances provided, although you will no doubt find yourself improvising to some extent. Like all appraisers and appraisees, you have less than complete information: you simply cannot know it all. The object of the exercise is to perform as an appraiser or appraisee and learn something about appraisal interviewing from this experience.

Finally, the roles are such that they can be played as either male or female.

Lord David Beaumont Primary School: general

The school is a group 6 all-through primary school serving the mainly residential area of Beaumont Green, a suburb of Didby.

Since 1980, a very real element of competition has developed between the schools, less through the desire of the headteachers than through the pressure of parents. All of the schools have had to put aside much time to show prospective parents around, and transfers between schools are on the increase. One likely result is that Lord David Beaumont and Kemsal Rise Schools will be oversubscribed for next September.

Pat Lasalle, the head, is well known in the community. Generally staff, parents and governors are supportive of efforts to modernize the image of the school. Pat has shown interest in curriculum reform, INSET, management training and appraisal. A few dissenters have suggested that things

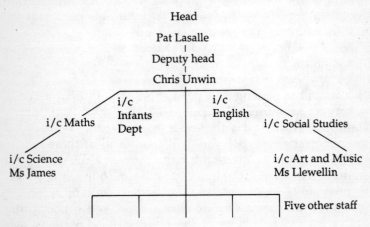

Figure AII.1 *The organization of Lord David Beaumont Primary School*

move too fast, consultation is not all it should be and important information is not always passed on to staff.

Figure AII.1 summarizes the school's staff structure.

Case study: Chris Unwin, deputy head

General brief

Chris is 50 and will have been at the school for fifteen years at the start of next (summer) term. Now lives alone (since spouse, who was a teacher at the local comprehensive school, died three years ago) and seems to have developed an increasing interest in country life (wine-making, keeping chickens, small-scale horticulture). Also a keen animal lover with three cats and two dogs.

Originally a career teacher with clear sights on a headship. Applied for the post as head of Lord David Beaumont three years ago when the present head was appointed and was frustrated at not being interviewed. The bereavement shortly afterwards resulted in an apparent loss of motivation.

Apart from teaching, specific responsibilities are for school finance and school visits. Classroom work is recognized as good, and Chris devotes much time to displaying the class's work in the classroom and around the school.

When the head is out of school, Chris is in charge. A potentially difficult situation arose recently. A father turned up wanting to see his daughter, and Chris permitted this. The family had split up, and a recent national news item concerning child abduction from a school had made heads very wary about this.

The school's accounts are well kept, and Chris confirms that the school is always short of the resources asked for by colleagues. There has been a recent disagreement about allocation between Chris and Terri Llewellin (i/c Art and Music).

The school was involved in two visits last year. Ms James (Science) took her class to the County Show, and the younger 4th year group, taught by Ms Reeves, went to Offley Hall, the LEA's residential centre.

Chris Unwin is regarded well by 4th year parents and has been able to use knowledge of the comprehensive school to ease their fears about transfer.

Subject brief

Generally you enjoy your work at the school and feel well on top of it. School provides some antedote to the quiet life you lead in your cottage. You are prepared to do your share of extra tasks but have now given up hopes of a headship and enjoy the kind of life you lead away from school.

You believe that your thirty years experience in primary schools has made you a good teacher and you are not unhappy to be labelled traditional. The children both like and respect you and you get good work out of most of them. You have seen curriculum innovation come and go and the latest round will be no different. These management courses, which the head has brought to your attention on more than one occasion, are for the younger less experienced deputies, and anyway the residential element is out of the question because of the animals at home.

You recall the afternoon you were left in charge and Mr Doberman had turned up wanting to see his daughter Sarah about a change of arrangement for after school. You had brought the second-year girl to the foyer and, fortunately, saw father and daughter together in your office. Later the school secretary told you the Dobermans had split up and that Mr Doberman had no access to his daughter. You had breathed a sigh of relief that you had not left father and daughter alone by the exit door! You had mentioned this specific incident to Pat Lasalle, expressing the view that such difficult family circumstances should be known more widely by the staff, and he said he would give some thought to this problem.

There had been an uncomfortable incident last week which related to your specific responsibilities. Terri Llewellin (i/c Art and Music) had handled her disagreement with you over the proposed allocation of money for the next financial year very dramatically.

Terri believed that it was time Art took more of a 'natural' place in the curriculum: creative work should derive from other curriculum activities which so often acted as a stimulus. She quoted the 4th year English topic on the sea as a case in point. Such a change would require her to take fewer specialist lessons and her colleagues to do more art in conjunction with their other work. Most seemed willing enough but needed some in-service training and extra materials for their rooms. Terri had been to see the head, who stressed that the allocations of resources were 'proposed' only, and depended on receipt of further information from County. However, you understand, that the head had said he would support her case for additional funding from the current budget.

Case study: Pat Lasalle

Appraiser's brief

Lord David Beaumont Primary School is doing well in terms of parental choice, your relationship with the governors is very good and you feel you have retained your grip on the school. There have been niggles between staff on occasions this year, but the ease with which your scheme for appraisal went through in December indicates that the staff are generally contented with the way you run the school. Other colleague heads have found appraisal to be something of a minefield. You were, however, disappointed at Chris Unwin's lack of support for the idea; although not opposing it, there was not a lot of enthusiasm.

Chris had done well enough in exercising specific responsibilities but a difficulty over finance had arisen this year. Ms Llewellin had been very convincing about the role of art in primary education when she spoke to you after her course, and she had been very upset when she failed to secure the promise of more money from Chris for the coming year.

Chris has told you what the priorities for spending for next year should be. They are that Science should receive an extra injection of funds again this year to complete the curriculum development plans, in line with County guidelines; a little extra should go towards the purchase of computer software now available for social studies. Other curriculum areas would receive the usual allocations to keep them ticking over. However, you feel there is a case for more funding for Art, as proposed by Ms Llewellin.

You had been considering two issues raised by Chris in the course of the year. The first was the sharing of information about pupil's family circumstances, and you were concerned about confidentiality in cases like the Dobermans. Chris had remained in the office with Mr Doberman and Sarah, but perhaps the father ought to have been questioned more closely before getting Sarah from class?

One thought that you would wish to raise with Chris concerned trips; Kemsal Rise School had an annual visit to France, which had received coverage in the local press. Lord David Beaumont, by comparison, was doing very little.

Finally, there is the problem of INSET and management courses. Chris, although suggesting that they may be valuable for others, steadfastly refuses to go on anything with a residential element. You feel it is time this problem was faced head-on.

References

Abbs, P. (1974) *Autobiography in Education*. London, Heinemann.

ACAS (1986) *Report of Working Group on Appraisal/Training*. London, Advisory, Conciliation and Arbitration Service, June 1986.

Bessell, R. (1971) *Interviewing and Counselling*. London, Batsford.

Boehm, A.E. and Weinberg, R.A. (1977) *The Classroom Observer: A Guide for Developing Observation Skills*. New York, Teachers College Press.

Boydell, T. and Pedler, R. (1981) *Management Self-Development: Concepts and Practices*. Farnborough, Gower.

Cross, C.P. (1974) *Interviewing and Communication in Social Work*. Routledge & Kegan Paul.

Bunnell, S. (1987) *Teacher Appraisal in Practice*. London, Heinemann.

DES (1986) *Better Schools, Evaluation and Appraisal*. Proceedings of Conference at Birmingham, November 1985. London, HMSO.

Elliott-Kemp, J. (1986) *SIGMA: A Process-Based Approach to Staff Development*. Sheffield City Polytechnic, PAVIC Publications.

Elliott-Kemp, J. and Rogers, C. (1982) *The Effective Teacher: A Person-Centred Development Guide*. Sheffield City Polytechnic, PAVIC Publications.

Fidler, B. and Cooper, R. (eds.; (1988) *Staff Appraisal in Schools and Colleges*, Harlow, Longman.

Graham, D. (1985) *Those Having Torches . . . Teacher Appraisal: A Study*. Ipswich, Suffolk Education Department.

——(1987) *In the Light of Torches. Teacher Appraisal. A Further Study*. Ipswich, Suffolk Education Department.

Hewton, E.W. (1988a) *School-Focused Staff Development: Guidelines for Policymakers.* Basingstoke, Falmer Press.

Hewton, E. (1988b) Appraisal: the present position. *Education,* 8 January.

Hobbs, T. (1987) Training in basic counselling and communication skills: a workshop format. In Open University Coping with Crisis Research Group (eds.) *Running Workshops.* London, Croom Helm.

Ivey, A. and Gluckstern, B. (1977) *Basic Attending Skills,* Amherst, Microtraining Associates.

Long, P. (1986) *Performance Appraisal Revisited,* Third IPM, Survey. London, Institute of Personnel Management.

NDC (1988) *Appraisal Supplement to Annotated Bibliography No. 1.* 2nd Edition compiled by BS Niblett. Bristol, National Development Centre for School Management Training.

Randell, G., Packard,. P. and Slater, J. (1984) *Staff Appraisal.* London, Institute of Personnel Management.

Rudduck, J. (ed.) (1982) *Teachers in Partnership: Four Studies of In-Service Collaboration.* York, Longmans/SCDC.

Stubbs, M. and Delamont, S. (1976) (eds.) *Explorations in Classroom Observation.* London, Wiley.

Trethowan D. (1987) *Appraisal and Target Setting: A Handbook for Teacher Development.* London, Harper & Row.

Turner, G. and Clift, P. (1985) *A First Review and Register of School-Based Teacher Appraisal Schemes.* Milton Keynes, School of Education, Open University.

Walker, R. and Adeleman, C. (1975) *A Guide to Classroom Observation.* London, Methuen.

Wragg, E.C. (1987) *Teacher Appraisal: A Practical Guide.* Basingstoke, Macmillan.

Woodcock, M. and Francis, D. (1982) *The Unblocked Manager: A Practical Guide to Self-Development.* Aldershot, Gower.

Videotapes

Cambridgeshire County Council (1984) *The Appraisal Interview.* Personnel Dept, Shire Hall, Cambridge.

Gower Training Resources (1987) *Appraisal Skills.* Aldershot, Hants.

Newcastle LEA (1988) *Video Training Package* from Appraisal Centre, Kenton School, Newcastle upon Tyne.

Suffolk LEA (1988) *What's in it for me?* 3 videos and supporting
   literature. Focus in Education Ltd, Hampton Hill, Middlesex.
Trotman & Co. (1987) *Understanding Appraisal*. Richmond, Surrey.
Video Arts (1983) *How Am I Doing*. Oxford St, London.

Further reading

There is now a voluminous literature on appraisal. That included in
the References section forms only a sample. Much of the writing is
concerned with appraisal and performance review in industrial
settings, but a considerable number of books, papers and articles
have appeared in the past five years relating to the appraisal of
teachers. The serious student is advised to obtain the material given
in the References and to follow up further references from these.
Workshop organizers will feel reasonably well informed if they
become familiar with the following – all of which are fully refer-
enced. They are in alphabetical order according to author.

Bunnell, S. (ed) (1987) *Teacher Appraisal in Practice* is a symposium of
    papers and case studies which offers a comprehensive guide to
    many of the problems and solutions found by those who have
    already implemented and evaluated appraisal schemes in
    schools.
The proceedings of the conference '*Better Schools, Evaluation and
    Appraisal*' (DES 1986) places appraisal in the overall context of
    the evaluation of schools and teaching and contains papers from
    those representing differing standpoints. It also includes details
    of schemes already operating in a number of schools.
Fidler, B. and Cooper, R. (eds.) (1988) *Staff Appraisal in Schools and
    Colleges* is again a collection of papers mainly on current practices
    in schools but including some useful chapters on concepts and
    issues.
Graham, D. (1985, 1987), chairman of the Suffolk Education De-
    partment, DES-sponsored project on teacher appraisal offers
    two very informative books covering many aspects of the topic.

Those Having Torches . . . is based upon careful research and offers detailed information on the meaning and purpose of appraisal, schemes in operation in the United Kingdom and abroad and examples of documentation used. *In the Light of Torches* contains chapters on costs, headteacher appraisal, classroom observation and training. This also contains the full report of the ACAS Appraisal/Training Working Group which is essential reading for those following the developing situation nationally.

Hewton, E. (1988a) *Appraisal: The Present Position* details the events leading up to the current uncertain situation on the appraisal scene and explains some of the problems and dilemmas which face the national pilot schemes.

Randell, G., Packard, P. and Slater, J. (1984) *Staff Appraisal* provides a clear and useful discussion of the different purposes of appraisal but concentrates upon performance review. The book also contains a number of ideas on training for appraisal skills.

Trethowan, D. (1987) *Appraisal and Target Setting* considers a number of matters, including the role of management, setting up an appraisal scheme, documentation, the interview, appraising the head and appraisal training. But underlying all of these is the central principle of target setting.

Wragg, E.C. (1987) *Teacher Appraisal: A Practical Guide* considers the criteria for judging teachers but gives particular attention to the place of classroom observation in the appraisal process.

Other sources

Most of the teachers' associations have from time to time offered their members an analysis of the appraisal situation, sometimes combined with a policy statement. These generally provide valuable information on the appraisal debate and indicate how attitudes have changed and developed over the years. They are usually obtainable by writing to or phoning the associations' offices.

More recently the six pilot LEAs have started to produce materials which are often available free of charge. The documents are usually meant to help teachers in the LEAs concerned to understand what is happening locally or nationally. They therefore offer useful and up to date information as well as a discussion of key issues. The materials can usually be obtained from the offices of the pilot projects and the addresses are listed below together with that of the national steering group and the national evaluation project:

1 Croydon	Ms Maeve Willis, Project Director, Room 13, The Davidson Professional Centre, Davidson Road, Croydon CR0 6DD. Tel: 01 654 8168.
2 Cumbria	Mr Jim Jack, Project Director, Pilot Study for Teachers Appraisal, Education Department, 5 Portland Square, Carlisle CA1 1PV. Tel: 0228 23456 Ext 2089.
3 Newcastle	Mr Keith Ridyard, Project Coordinator, School Teacher Appraisal Pilot Project, Kenton School, Drayton Road, Newcastle upon Tyne NE3 3RU.
4 Salford	Ms Dallas Hackett, Project Officer, Advisory Section, Town Hall, Bexley Square, Salford M3 5LT. Tel: 061 832 9751 Ext 341.
5 Somerset	Mr Victor Gane, Project Coordinator, Somerset Teacher Review and Development Study, Somerset Education Centre, Friarn Annexe, Wembdon Road, Bridgwater, Somerset TA6 7DL. Tel: 0278 450346.
6 Suffolk	Mr David Penrose, Coordinator, School Teacher Appraisal Project, Room 303, County Education Office, St Andrew House, Grimwade St, Ipswich, Suffolk IP4 1LJ. Tel: 0473 230000 Ext. 4406.
National Steering Group	Mrs Agnes McMahon, National Development Centre for School Management Training, 35 Berkeley Square, Bristol BS8 1JA. Tel: 0272 303030 Ext. M391.
Evaluation Project	Mr Rob Bollington, Evaluation of School Teacher Appraisal Pilot Study, Cambridge Institute of Education, Shaftesbury Road, Cambridge CB2 2BX. Tel: 0223 69631 Ext. 233.

Reading for workshop participants

This is always a difficult decision for there is so much that is informative and helpful and generally so little time for those who will attend the workshop to devote to prior reading. Furthermore, there is the problem of cost and copyright to consider. Nevertheless, it is useful if participants can come with some understanding of the current appraisal debate and the following items may be helpful.

1   The ACAS agreement (ACAS 1986).
2   Any recent teacher association or appraisal pilot project statement.
    These documents are often obtainable without charge.
3   Appraisal: The Present Position (Hewton 1988). This four page digest is available from the journal 'Education' for 25p.

Index